GET IT TOGETHER BY 30

To our parents, who always recognized the wisdom of the old maxim, "Do what you love and the money will follow."

"If you get your act together by the time you're 30, you'll be set for the rest of your life."

—Prof. Paul Jefferson
Haverford College

CONTENTS

Introduction

Nobody really reads book introductions, so I'll make mine short.

You'd never believe how many of my friends laughed at me when I told them that I, at the age of 31, was coauthoring a book titled *Get It Together by 30*. In their minds, I hadn't yet made it; what nerve did I have advising other people on how to get there? To them, anyone who'd made it by 30 would be a multimillionaire living on a yacht off the coast of Monaco. Since I'm nowhere near owning my own home—let alone a yacht—they thought I was posing as someone I wasn't.

But the editors at AMACOM who'd asked Jay Heflin and me to compose this book knew something you are about to find out—and something I've since told my friends. Getting it together by 30 doesn't mean being rich by 30. Rather, it means that you're on your way to having a successful career trajectory that might lead you to actually get rich, or famous, or just as content as you want to be—at a "normal" pace.

My presumption is that a lot of people start their careers off incorrectly and never have a chance to get it together at all, let alone by 30. They don't take advantage of obvious opportunities; they neglect the small details that impress others; and they lack the necessary confidence to get ahead. So when 30 rolls around—and for those of you still years away from it, it comes very fast—they're nowhere near where they should be.

The purpose of this book is to keep you on the right path, to help you take the practical steps you must take to get from wherever you are to wherever you want to be by 30. The advice we offer is culled from other employment experts, as well as from our own experiences.

Keep in mind that this book cannot guarantee success. In fact, in some situations the advice might be far from applicable to your life. But we are convinced that for you and every other reader, we offer in the following pages a variety of sound, practical steps you can use now, today, to help advance your career.

As you probably know, when you're building a career, everyone under the sun will offer you advice. If the advice sounds good, take it. If not, just let it slide. And when you get into conversations with older people, ask them one question: How did you get started? If you like their stories, find out every detail you can. If you don't like them, find others. People like to talk about their successes, so tap as wide a number of people as you can get.

Jay and I can't tell you everyone's success story, but we can encourage you to track down the ones most closely linked to you, one by one, starting with family members and friends' older relatives. So read this book, and then get going!

—Richard Thau

GET IT TOGETHER BY 30

CHAPTER 1

It's Time to Grow Up: Jay Explains Why Rob Petrie Would Be on Unemployment Today

Do you remember rushing home from school, tossing your books into your bedroom, and flicking on the family TV set, just in time to catch the late-afternoon lineup of sitcom reruns? In my family room, after school each day, the ritual was always the same: Get the books out of sight, grab a snack, and park yourself in front of the set until dinner. It didn't matter what the lineup of reruns was; I loved all of them. Whether it was *I Love Lucy* or *The Munsters*, nothing was going to unglue my eyes from that set until the nightly news came on. That's when the grown-ups began their own television ritual and we children had to complete our homework.

I still remember my favorite sitcom picks from fifth grade. The lineup started with *Superman*. Next came *The Brady Bunch*. Then it was the Petrie clan on *The Dick Van Dyke Show*, followed by *I Dream of Jeannie*, with Barbara Eden's critically concealed belly button.

Personally, I thought the lineup peaked with the Bradys and Petries. My preadolescent scheming heart loved the way the Brady kids plotted their way out of their weekly predicament. And comedy-writer Rob's antics cracked me up every time; too bad they made fantasy-wife Laura so nervous. ("OOOhhh, Robbb!!")

To be candid, I never fully understood why *I Dream of Jeannie's* Major Nelson didn't quit NASA and set Jeannie up in Las Vegas with her own one-woman show. He could have called it *I Dream of Showgirl!* People would have paid big money to see her dance around a bottle — and the major would have made enough money to start his own space program. No more worrying about Dr. Bellows discovering Jeannie was a genie. Although you would think that a rocket scientist would know *something* was going on.

Which leads me to another notion I had about the show: Why *was* Jeannie's magic kept a secret from Dr. Bellows? To me as a kid, he seemed like a nice enough guy, and I'm sure he would have appreciated knowing Jeannie's secret. I mean, the good doctor feared for his sanity every time he bore witness to one of Jeannie's magical creations. I'm sure he would have been relieved to know he wasn't hallucinating or experiencing a nervous breakdown. In fact, knowing about Jeannie might have led him toward an inner peace and probably would have transformed him into a cooler, hipper doctor, one who wouldn't have been so stuffy and uptight. So even as a child, I had an inquiring mind!

Still, I developed a lot of preconceived notions about real life from TV. Some I was aware of right away, like my crush on Marcia Brady or Jeannie's possible success in Vegas. Others were more subtle and not realized for some time. On TV (before *Roseanne*) everyone had an interesting, fun, and well-paid job. As I watched fictional TV families, I began fantasizing about how life operated and what I should expect from it, especially in the area of work.

Subconsciously, as I partook in my afternoon ritual, Rob Petrie seemed secure in his job with the *Alan Brady Show*. Sure, Alan would threaten to fire Rob once in a while, but no one took it seriously; in fact, it added to the show. Mike Brady also seemed comfortable with his lifelong position at his architectural firm and showed no signs of stress from supporting six kids, one wife, a paid servant, and a mortgage. He never once scowled or had a discouraging word. The man was so carefree, in fact, that any of his dependents (or Sam, the butcher, for that matter) could barge into his study, at any time of the day, and unload their burden onto him. Anytime was quality time.

Needless to say, I was a little bit surprised when I became a part of the real, nonsitcom workforce. In all my years of watching these slice-of-life scenarios, I never once heard phrases like *cutbacks, forced retirement, career changes, office politics, underemployment, hierarchy disputes,* or *child care.*

Of course, TV wasn't my only source for learning about the job world; there were Mom and Dad. But still their situations seemed similar to what I saw on the tube. Each parent had a lifelong job that ended only when retirement was chosen, and that came with the security of a pension and Social Security benefits. My parents also could afford to purchase a house and have multiple family vacations throughout the year, features that are becoming harder to find with today's stagnating earnings and increased cost of living. That gravy train of financial and career security, so enjoyed by previous generations, is changing in our time: the time of Generation X.

But gloomy issues such as job security and wage reform affect only those of us who are employed. The yet-to-be-employed must contend with finding a job—not only one that they like, but one that will be around for a few years. And finding that type of job security is becoming increasingly difficult.

I do not think there was ever an episode, on any rerun I saw, where Major Nelson or Mike Brady came home, slammed down his car keys on the coffee table and said, "That's it, I hate that job. I don't care if I starve, or what Mom and Dad think, I'm outta there!!" Even if there was an episode like this one, it may not have made it past the censors.

But still, this type of scenario is more in line with what is happening with today's youth entering the workforce. In the '90s, people are seeing the jobs that they are offered and not liking much about them. One reason for this is that many people didn't really consider what they wanted in a career before they entered college or postsecondary school. When they graduated with a major that left them totally unemployable, they got stuck with what was out there.

In today's world, with all the changes taking place within the labor force, people must ask themselves several probing, heartfelt questions to find out exactly what turns them on in a career. The job situations of yesterday, the ones found on the TV reruns we all loved so much, are gone or becoming extinct. A Rob Petrie of today doesn't worry about being let go because of something his wife said to his boss. (Remember the toupee episode?) Rather, Rob Petries may become obsolete because of technology or lower-wage foreign competition, and that is *really* something to worry about.

Nowadays, a person is better off being more like Sergeant Joe Friday from *Dragnet*. His phrase, "Just the facts, ma'am," is something you will be telling yourself a lot if you want to wind up in a career that fits you and is one that will be around until you retire.

Well, getting the facts that will help you decide on the right career for you is a major thrust of this book. The pages that follow contain information to absorb and questions to ask yourself that will assist you in finding the right road for your career. In beginning this trip, the only skill you have to have is being honest with yourself. Be unfailingly honest while answering the questions laid out in the book, while applying those answers to the information about the future of work (also within these pages). Your reward will be to discover what career is best for you and how to approach that career from an educational standpoint.

Having a clear picture of what you want out of a career will be key for you. But no matter what job choice you make, the pages that follow will guide you through your decision—and, by using this information, you will be well on your way to getting it together by 30!

CHAPTER 2

Your Career: It's Not Just a Job, It's a Reality

"Know thyself." This inscription at the Delphi Oracle makes just as much sense now as it did thousands of years ago.

Have you ever heard the saying, "Whoever has the most toys wins"? For someone we know, it was his motto all through college. He believed that if the money was right, he'd be happy with any job. Needless to say, after graduation, he took the job that offered him the highest starting salary . . . and, after loathing his work routine, quit it within a year.

"On Sunday nights, I started to dread having to go into work on Monday," he said. "Soon I began dreading work on Sunday afternoons. The money just didn't matter after a while," he admitted. "I mean, when you're sitting at a desk, hating what you're doing, money is no motivation to get the job done correctly. You just want to get the task over with, as fast as possible, so it's out of your hair."

Heed this motto and what our friend experienced. Certainly it's true that money is important; anyone who tells you different is trying to sell you something. But a balance must be struck between doing what you want to do with your career and having the type of lifestyle that you want to lead. Common sense will tell you that it takes a certain level of income to enjoy even the most basic middle-class lifestyle. Even the simplest of tastes can only be sustained by a positive cash flow. But be careful: Tipping the scales of your lifestyle desires against your job choice—in one direction or the other—can lead to an unfulfilled way of life.

The best way to guard against this pitfall is to know yourself. To truly see what turns you on and off not only will allow you to make better, informed choices about the type of career you desire, but also will give you insight into the lifestyle that actually fits you best.

We're sure, with so many of us being TV enthusiasts, we remember rerun episodes of the '50s sitcom *The Honeymooners*. It is safe to say that the character of Ralph Kramden (played by Jackie Gleason), who was a hot-tempered bus driver, did not know himself very well. If he had, he probably would have quit the New York City Transit Authority and taken up professional wrestling (that sort of temper works well in the ring, but not behind the wheel of a bus).

Now, of course, Ralph Kramden's flareups are what made the show so interesting and funny, not to mention a part of classic television. But in reality that is no way to go through life. Imagine someone being that high-strung and having to navigate through New York City traffic, day in and day out: Do the words *human time bomb* come to mind?

Fortunately, we have progressed beyond the time where just having a job is satisfactory for everyone. Today's jobs define who we are and give insightful hints to others about our self-perception. When meeting strangers, a common first question is, "What do you do for a living?" Some people, satisfied with their present employment, will talk at great length about the work they do. Others, those not fulfilled and without a clue as to why, will usually give a brief description and hope that the topic soon shifts to something else.

What would you rather be: the enthusiastic talker or the shy, shrinking violet?

How do you find out what turns you on in the area of careers? Does the tooth fairy whisper it into your ear as she's lifting your last baby tooth? ("Here's a quarter for the tooth, Johnny, and by the way, your career choice is in the field of electronics. Specialize in stereo receivers.") Or do your parents lecture you about what they know you should do, to the point where all other career choices are drowned out? Or does something strike you, like lightning, with the revelation of your dream job?

Clearly this is not how jobs—at least the most appropriate ones—are chosen. Instead, the answer comes from within the individual, after long and thorough consideration. No one can tell you what you want to be.

On the next page is a list of questions that you can ask yourself, questions that will allow you to see what your likes are and what interests could lead to a career choice. When reading over these questions, it's important not to block any answers. There are no wrong or silly responses; all of your personal interests, no matter how absurd they might sound, can lead to some spot in the workplace.

An example of someone with an absurd hobby leading to a career is the actor (and multimillionaire) Jim Carrey. As a child he used to entertain himself for hours with his favorite hobby: making funny faces. His mother used to try to stop him from doing this; she viewed it as a waste of time. In the end, this hobby was anything but a waste. National, well-respected film critics deem him a creative genius because of those contortions he makes with his face. I'm sure Mom is very proud and very happy that son Jim did not take her advice.

So take a look at these soul-searching, interest-provoking questions and be honest with yourself. No one has to know what your answers are; in fact, you don't even have to write them down. But keep in mind that these questions will help you achieve an idea about the career of your dreams only if you answer them seriously.

Personal Interest Questions

- What do I look forward to doing in my free or work time?
- What gives me a sense of accomplishment?
- What kind of jobs do I respect?
- How do I picture myself living a few years from now? (In a house? With a car? Traveling a lot?)
- What tasks do I have for myself today? (Delivering newspapers? Cutting the grass?) Do I enjoy any of these tasks?
- What do I like about my tasks?
- Apart from my tasks, where else do I get the most sense of satisfaction by performing some necessary ritual?
- Deep down, in my gut, is there a job I've never told a soul about that I think I could do well?

These questions are just the beginning of a series of questions that you should be asking about yourself. From here, other questions should spring forward. With each new question that arises, take it seriously and answer it as honestly as you can. Remember, never mind if it's a silly answer, in the end there is nothing silly about making money doing something you love.

Still not having a sense of what you enjoy doing? That's all right. Here are some more questions that can help point you in the right direction.

More Personal Interest Questions

- Do you enjoy working with your hands?
- What subjects interest you? Why?
- What do you watch on TV? Do you ever think you could be doing what certain characters are doing? Which characters are those?
- Do you ever stop to think about the process behind something, such as a building being constructed or a movie being filmed?
- Do you look forward to logging on to the Internet? Where do you go when you're surfing around the World Wide Web? Your roaming should tell you something.
- Where are you when time seems to pass quickly? Is it while you're shooting hoops, working on a car, knitting a sweater, or typing on the computer?
- Do you look forward to seeing friends at school or at your job? Do you enjoy your time alone and feel that so much more can be accomplished when no one else is around?
- Do you need to see the product of your labors daily, or are you comfortable working on long-term projects where, after weeks or months of labor, there is a single, large payoff?
- Is money always on your mind? Are you always thinking of ways to make it that no one else has come up with yet?
- Does it make you feel good when you help others?
- Do you like being the leader of group projects, or do you enjoy it more when others are in charge?
- Do you enjoy making people laugh? Do you like being the center of attention?
- Do you like to organize the items in your bedroom? Do you dislike it when things are messy around you?
- Would you like to live in a big city, or, would you prefer a small town? Do you like doing things at a slow, relaxed pace, or does the hustle of being rushed excite you?
- Do you start and finish projects on your own? Did you often have a lemonade stand or a paper route as a kid?
- Do you like getting up early to enjoy a morning, or do you love to sleep in?
- Do you enjoy working on the details of a project, or do you look more at the big picture?
- Is life more fun when you know what is coming and things are more secure, or do you like to find out about things as they come along?

All these questions should begin to get you thinking about what you like and dislike about your present life. From here you can begin to plot what your next move should be. If college is your next step and, after reading these questions, you find out that you like a more secure environment to work in, then accounting or pharmacy might be a job choice for you. If you enjoy working with your hands and like to see what you've accomplished at the end of a day, then perhaps construction work might be your game. These questions are designed to indicate what jobs you might like to do for a career, on the basis of what you enjoy doing today.

It's very important, especially at the beginning of your career search, to know yourself. One way of getting to know yourself is to ask yourself questions. The other way is to ask others about how they see you. Talk to your close friends, family members, and school faculty—people you respect. Ask them about what they would see you enjoying as a career. Sometimes the best way to get to know ourselves and see ourselves for what we truly are is through the opinions of those people who are closest to us.

CHAPTER 3

It *Is* What You Know: The Link Between Education and Employment

Being competitive and securing your place in tomorrow's markets will boil down to two things: what you know and whom you know. We'll get to the latter elsewhere in the book. In the meantime, let's talk about education, something that has been increasing in importance since the turn of the last century, and a requirement more vital to job security than ever before.

The biggest increases in job opportunities for the next century are the ones that will require a college degree. From the years 1994 to 2005, according to Bureau of Labor Statistics (BLS) projections, positions of this kind are expected to increase 27 percent. In contrast, jobs that will *not* require any postsecondary education should increase by just 5 percent. What all this information boils down to is this: If you want to get ahead, you must get a college degree.

To give you some point of reference for how degrees are becoming increasingly important, think about Abraham Lincoln. He became a lawyer by simply working in a law office. Today, in most states, not only do lawyers have to excel in their undergraduate studies to get accepted by a law school, but after graduating from law school they must also pass a grueling bar exam before ever representing a client.

Needing a postsecondary degree is not just limited to white-collar professionals. Many expert blue-collar workers also need a postsecondary education. Since computers are now being installed in car engines, auto mechanics must have knowledge about such devices. A good way for them to learn about the latest technology is through vocational schools. Of course, tuition is not cheap for these schools, but they are becoming more and more popular, simply because there is an increasing need for what they teach.

So no matter what area of expertise you're considering, some sort of postsecondary school training will be necessary for you to secure a job. Obtaining this degree will pay off—literally. As history has proved, as the need for a higher-educated employee rises, so does the salary. Also, most workers who are educated get the most choices in job availability and work locations, not just salary. Clearly, in the job arena, the more you learn, the better you earn.

As projected by the BLS, job opportunities in the United States that require a master's degree will increase the most for the period between 1994 and 2005. Jobs that require only on-the-job training will have the slowest growth in hiring. The table on the next page shows the *percentage* increases for various categories of degrees and/or training. (Note that the percentages are calculated by comparing each educational/training category in 1994 with its *own* projected figure for 2005, *not* with the entire pool. Thus the "28%" across from "Master's degree" means that for every 100 jobs available for a person

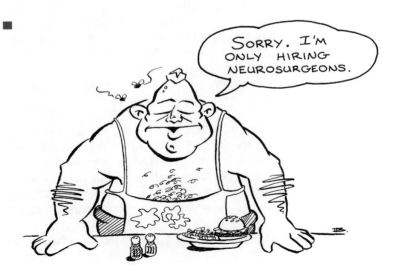

Percentage Increases in Hiring With the Following Degrees or Training, 1994–2005

Degree or Training	Percentage Increase
Master's degree	28%
Bachelor's degree	27
Associate degree	24
First professional degree	22
Doctoral degree	18
Work experience plus a bachelor's degree	16
Work experience	13
Short-term on-the-job-training	13
Post-secondary vocational training	11
Long-term on-the-job-training	10
Moderate-term on-the-job-training	5

with a master's degree in 1994, there will be 128 in 2005—*not* that 28 percent of the workforce will need master's degrees.)

The table on page 14, also from the BLS, shows the projected *numerical* increases in various educational/training categories.

A casual reader of these statistics might conclude that jobs requiring only short-term on-the-job training are the ones to aspire to because they will be so plentiful. But that would be shortsighted and wholly wrong. There will be many of these jobs, yes, but they're likely to be low-paying and dead-end.

To explore the changing job environment, *The New York Times* ran a series of articles in early 1996 that dealt with the notion of job shock. People making six figures a year were suddenly out of a job and clueless about what to do to remedy their situations. Some of them had

Numerical Increases in Hiring With the Following Degrees or Training, 1994-2005

Degree or Training	Increased Job Opportunities (in Numbers)
First professional degree	+374,000
Doctoral degree	+180,000
Master's degree	+427,000
Work experience, plus a bachelor's or higher degree	+3,764,000
Bachelor's degree	+1,303,000
Associate degree	+963,000
Post-secondary vocational training	+743,000
Work experience	+1,331,000
Long-term on-the-job training	+1,229,000
Moderate-term on-the-job training	+864,000
Short-term on-the-job training	+6,513,000

to take menial jobs just to pay their bills. You see, most of these people were in middle-management positions, and that layer of corporate America is becoming ever thinner.

This information is not being cited as a scare tactic, but rather to make you realize that if you choose the wrong career path it may affect you several years down the road. And then it might be difficult for you to afford the time and the money that it will take to get retrained.

CHAPTER 4

Pick a Degree, Any Degree?

Now that you have some sort of insight into what your interests are, it's time to start looking at what jobs are available to match those interests. Even for high school readers, this section will be valuable because it's never too soon to start thinking about your career, one that likely will last several decades.

As the first section indicated, most employers in the twenty-first century will be expecting their job candidates to hold a college degree. Even jobs for which a college degree is not necessary today will soon be open only to those who have that little, but very important, piece of paper in their hands.

Based on what field of expertise you wish to pursue, the following will instruct you as to which postsecondary education establishment is the next right step for you. As postsecondary schools go, there are generally five ways of pursuing such an education:

1. Vocational school degree
2. Undergraduate or college degree
3. MBA degree
4. Other graduate degree
5. Continuing education

All these different types of degrees allow the student to pursue different opportunities. Listed below are the degrees and the types of jobs usually associated with obtaining them, as listed in Carol Kleiman's book *The Best Jobs for the 1990s and Beyond.*

<u>Vocational Degree</u>

Some Job Examples: Mechanics, repairers, cosmetologists, computer programmers, aircraft technicians, drafters, travel agents, hotel personnel

* Word of warning: Financial columnist Jane Bryant Quinn advises checking into a vocational school's reputation. She says, "[Some vocational schools] are bleeding millions of dollars from the federal program for guaranteed student loans . . . .They sign up poorly educated, unqualified students by promising them brilliant futures . . . . Students take to loans to pay for their 'education' but soon discover they can't do the work . . . so they drop out, with nothing to show for their hopes and efforts but a debt they can't pay back."

Kleiman urges the potential vocational student to ask, "Who are the teachers? What are their credentials? What is the school's placement rate? Do they return all or a portion of your money if you withdraw?" These types of questions should be answered before any contract is signed with the school.

<u>Undergraduate or College Degree</u>

Some Job Examples: Computer software companies, advertising agencies, banks, law offices, consulting, technical jobs, public relations, sales and brokerage firms, entertainment industry

* Changing tide: Corporate America used to heavily recruit people with business degrees. Now, as times are changing, so is the degree preference. For most companies, the choice in hiring seems to be for people who have a degree in the liberal arts. Companies are looking for a more well-rounded employee who possesses traits such as creativity, interpersonal skills, and adaptability, not just knowledge of macroeconomics. Funny how times change; a few years ago a liberal arts degree was another word for being unemployed or at best underemployed.

<u>MBA Degree</u>

Some Job Examples: Movers and shakers of corporate America, the future CEOs and board chairmen: the corner-office people

* Keeping with the times: People possessing MBAs are now becoming more and more popular to hire, for the reasons stated above. Having an MBA degree is also a way to secure an employed position within tomorrow's workforce.

Other Graduate Degree

Some Job Examples: Social workers, librarians, accountants, managers, human resources personnel, journalists, architects, landscape experts, business and financial executives

* Winning combination: Once again, having a mix in education of humanities and business will serve you well in these work situations, just as having an undergraduate degree does.

Continuing Education Programs

Some Job Examples: Almost everyone at every level in the workplace. Most are studying foreign languages in anticipation of the world market; others are learning more about computers.

* Continuing trend: According to Kleiman, "People are investing time and money [in continuing education programs] because they know it will pay off in the future, and it will." Kleiman reports that "nearly one in four major companies—double the number in 1982—requires upper-middle and senior executives to participate in a continuing education program."

Even though education is increasing in importance, the most significant ingredient to any business venture is the individual. What you do with the strengths and weaknesses you are given will determine what you make of your life. Earning a degree, from no matter what area, will only enhance what you already have inside you. Remember, having a degree or not having one doesn't make you a success or a failure; what you do is what will count in the end.

Just a few months before I graduated from college, I met with an alumnus who was working for a magazine in New York City. He was sixteen years my senior, and I arranged to meet with him because I was thinking about entering the publishing field.

The experience was one that I'll never forget. He worked in a subterranean office on the Upper West Side, and there were no windows at all. We sat across from each other, alongside his cluttered desk.

In his basement that day he basically presented me with reality.

What he said was this: "You're graduating from an excellent, small, liberal arts college. No one outside of the school's immediate area has heard of it. Don't expect the school's name to get you a job. Rather, what will get you a job is the confidence and intelligence that you developed while at the school."

"Also," he said, "if you want to enter the writing field, you have to have a burning desire to tell the world something it isn't hearing already. And you should express it in a way that no one is expressing it. Otherwise, you should think about another career."

The last thing he said was that I should enjoy the final weeks of college (I had about two months left at the time). "Sit under a tree. Watch the sun set. Listen to music. Enjoy these last several weeks, because you'll never have it this good again."

Sobering, but looking back on it, probably true.

Even when you have decided what career you would like to learn about based on your interest, remember, no decision is written in stone. If, once you start learning about the career, you find it not to your liking, switch majors—or even schools—if you're not happy with your course of action. Finding out what majors or schools are right for you might take some time: Take it. Remember, you're allowed a number of false starts, but too many and it begins to count against you. Errors become harder to correct as you move along the time line.

There is a theory that says, "It doesn't matter what you major in; just get the degree." That idea is fine if you have no idea what career you're considering after graduation. History majors, for example, have few clear options in this discipline; they can become professors or teachers, and that's about it. But history majors, like others in the liberal arts world, can choose from any number of careers unrelated to history where the employers seek the person's capacity to reason, think, and be articulate, not to recite the signatories to the Treaty of Ghent.

BORED? TIRED OF THAT OLD JOB? THEN WHY NOT BECOME A NEUROPSYCHOLOGIST AT "DICK + DICK'S SCHOOL OF NEUROPSYCHOLOGY AND GUN REPAIR"! FOR ONLY $99.95 YOU TOO CAN BECOME A NEUROPSYCHOLOGIST IN ONLY THREE MONTHS!
WE ACCEPT FOOD STAMPS!

CHAPTER 5

Internships: Don't Want to Commit? You're Free to Quit

We're sure at this point you're probably saying to yourself, "OK, I know what I enjoy and don't enjoy doing, and I know what type of postsecondary school is right for me. But what I really want to know about my possible career choice is whether I will actually like it."

This is a sensible concern, considering that you will spend at least one-third of your adult life earning a living. So how do you find out whether you will enjoy the career you picked? It's easy: Try it out by doing an internship. In the world of real estate, the three most important words are *location, location, location*. In career decision making, the three most important words are *internships, internships, internships.*

Interns are uaually students working in business environments. Internships enable you to get hands-on experience in the career of your choice. Often an internship for a college student will last a semester (three months), and the student may earn college credit, instead of money, that is applied toward requirements for graduation.

People, both on the college and professional side, are hailing the virtues of internships. In fact, according to the National Society for Experiential Education, internships have become so popular that they have increased approximately 37 percent since 1991. This type of employment trend is clearly becoming a standard step in the career process.

Corporate internship programs allow companies to pay minimal salaries to the students in the program, thereby gaining near-free labor. In fact, many internships around the country don't offer any sort of benefits or monetary gain for the intern at all. What is provided is experience.

In today's increasingly competitive economy, many firms can no longer afford to spend valuable time and money on unknown quantities. Internships allow a company to test the prospective employee, nearly risk-free. A lot more can be learned about a person's work habits and personal attributes during a semester of working on the job than from a whole slew of half-hour interviews. It actually pays the company, through seeing what type of employee the student will be, to have interns around, rather than spending money having the human resources department scout all over the country looking for new employees. Internships lure the want-to-be employees to the company instead of vice versa.

This may sound like slave labor. What many internships boil down to is doing menial tasks for no money. Sure, some interns may actually get the chance to do something interesting, but that will come after swallowing their pride and making the coffee, delivering the mail, and running errands. Is this humbling experience worth it? Most definitely.

In a recent article from *USA Today*, Telia Cummings talks about her experience while working on the ABC television show *Nightline*. "The twelve-week internship cost me about $1,500, including $150 to the University of Akron in Ohio, to administer my one-credit internship. I also paid $15 to $25 a week for subways from downtown Washington to the Maryland suburbs."

Cummings said she had to skimp on a lot of necessities, was dependent on her friends' generosity a few times for loans, and took full advantage of leftovers from *Nightline's* catered dinners on Thursdays. But, she says, after all the expense and trouble, it was, without a doubt, worth the time.

She saw this opportunity as being a once-in-a-lifetime chance to work with some of the biggest names in an industry that she wished to pursue. Working at *Nightline* only strengthened her desire to continue in the media industry. Cummings also realized that getting professional experience—no matter what her duties were—would make her more attractive to employers once she started interviewing for permanent work. She couldn't be more on target. Having some sort of internship experience is one of the main items a hiring human resources director will look for when screening a candidate's resume.

"Had I not done that internship, I certainly would never be where I am today—or even gotten my first job," proclaims Steve Schanwald in a recent *Chicago Tribune* article. According to the piece, Schanwald is the marketing and broadcasting director for the Chicago Bulls. During his college days, Schanwald worked as a summer intern—for free—for the University of Maryland's sports marketing department. His friends thought the department was taking advantage of Steve because he was working without being paid.

But, as fate would prove, the internship paid a wonderful dividend. Schanwald's first job after college ended up being with the U.S. Air Force Academy as director of sports promotion. Suffice it to say, Schanwald's friends no longer saw a nonpaying internship as valueless.

Actually, thinking that nonpaying internships are a form of abuse is entirely shortsighted. Most interns, upon graduation, get more money from their first-time employer because they have had some experience, and experience is what usually determines the salary people will receive from their employers. As pointed out by Maury Hanigan, president of Hanigan Consulting, a New York firm that studies the internship programs of Fortune 500 companies, "College graduates who [have worked in] internship programs receive, on average, higher starting salaries and more job offers that those with no internship experience."

Keep in mind what the internship sponsor can offer in lieu of monetary payment. First, the sponsor can help you find employment after your graduation from college. A conscientious sponsor will want to return the favor of the intern's free labor, and is often well suited to doing this by opening his Rolodex and finding you a job. Moreover, the sponsor is a great reference if you need someone to tout your strengths and dedication to a prospective paid employer.

Some of the most important internships are those where you discover you are ill suited to an industry you thought you'd like. The reason this is a positive rather than a negative is simple: Interning gives you the ability to make major decisions at marginal cost.

Imagine, for example, that you're interested in two unrelated fields: botany and architecture. You take an internship with a botanist and find you really don't like flowers very much. Then you intern at an architectural firm, and decide that it's the right career path for you. Even though you didn't like botany, there was no commitment established there, and you could always say you tried it. The botanist lost nothing of value by having you around for a short while; in fact, she got your low-cost labor, and you got to try something new.

Imagine, though, that you graduate from college and have never interned. After months of searching, you find a job with a botanist, but three months later you are miserable and desperately want out. Unfortunately, you are stuck having to choose between keeping a job you hate or holding no job at all. In bed at night you keep wondering, "Why didn't I take a job in architecture?" and "Would I like that any better?"

Finally, you decide you want to jump from botany to architecture. "Will it look bad on my resume if I switch fields after a few months?" you ask yourself.

Yes, it will.

"Will it be hard for me to look for a new job while holding this one?" you also ask.

Yes, very hard.

So even if you find a job in architecture after a long search, the whole trouble of switching this way has been a major pain in the neck.

You'd have served yourself better by experimenting with an internship.

CHAPTER 6

Finding an Internship

Starting as an intern in a corporation and later becoming a full-time employee there is not uncommon. In fact, some reports show that as many as 80 percent of interns will be asked to join that company after graduating from postsecondary school.

Don't think that you're going to waltz right in to the company of your dreams and pick up an internship that carries you right to a secure, full-time position just as easily as cruising through the drive-in window of your favorite fast-food joint and picking up a burger. Be prepared for some fierce competition when interviewing for an internship slot. Remember, when it comes to getting any type of professional work, it's a buyer's market. The corporations are the choosy customers, and we are the meat they are scrutinizing for purchase.

Just as the number of internship programs are increasing, so are the students wishing to become a part of them. This tightening allows companies a greater choice when deciding who will work as an intern for their firm. The same *Chicago Tribune* article mentioned in Chapter 5 states that "for Motorola's six internships in its Northbrook-based Automotive and Industrial group, more than five hundred engineering students applied."

The article continues to say, "Kraft recruiters interviewed one hundred fifty candidates for eleven Kraft USA marketing spots." And, "Sidley and Austin received more than 1,000 resumes and coordinated

500 law school on-campus interviews for 47 jobs." Needless to say, the internship market is about the same as the job market: thick on candidates, thin on openings.

Let's face it: It's a tough world out there, no matter what you're trying to break into. In situations like these, it would be nice to have a family member owning the exact type of company that you wish to work for. However, if that were the case, you would not need this book and, therefore, would not be reading this sentence right now. So you'll have to plug along through the rest of these pages to find out what to do next.

To increase your chances of getting an internship (or a job for that matter), you must sell what you do best. You must accentuate your positives. This "accentuating" is exactly what will get you not only in the door but also in the employee chair. Selling what you do best is the only way to look for work, simply because it increases your chances of getting hired. A football coach doesn't send out his best quarterback to catch passes; that would be no way to win the game.

Not all companies seek only the students with the highest grades for their internship programs. "Good grades and related job experience are important, but we also look at what school activities they [the prospective interns] participate in," says Kim Hendershot, a personnel specialist at Burns and McDonell, located in Kansas City, Missouri. Her company is an engineering consulting firm that hires approximately 20 interns for paid positions throughout the year.

Hendershot says school activities are so important because they give an insight into what the student is about: Is he outgoing? Is she a team player? Is she a good leader? Can she adjust to changing situations? These questions are very important for a company to ask when deciding whom to hire, and they cannot be answered simply by a numerical standing, known as your grade point average. "Belonging to the Greek system or being a member of an organization can, a lot of times, tell us more about a student than can be reflected in their grades," says Hendershot.

On the next page you will find other attributes corporate sponsors say are important in their hiring considerations. But remember, this list is not complete. There are as many different qualities that are worth being hired for as there are corporations in America.

Positives That Can Get You an Internship

Positive attitude
Friendly, fun personality
Deep interest in or passion for the corporation's products or causes
Personal hobbies or interests
Extracurricular activities
Major
Flexibility with time availability
Background or experience in a related field
Feeling driven to accomplish tasks
Mature thinking
Eagerness to help others
Ability to work for little or no pay

Where does one go to find an internship? They are not listed in the want ads, and if you approached headhunters (professionally known as executive searchers), they would probably laugh in your face. (Headhunters work off a commission from the salary of the job they secure for their client. Internships pay next to nothing, or nothing at all; so by placing you in one, the headhunter would be working for free. It doesn't happen.)

You have to know where internships are located before you can get one. Most people find out about internships at their school placement offices. Such places usually house a lot of information on the subject. But beware: Many of the career placement offices throughout the country limit their listings of internship programs to the Fortune 500-size companies. What if that is not the type of internship that you are seeking? Go to your nearest library or bookstore and get hold of at least one the following:

Gilbert, Sara Dulaney. *Arco: Internships*. New York: Macmillan, 1995.
Krannich, Ronald L., and Krannich, Caryl. *The Directory of Federal Jobs and Employers*. Manassas Park, Va.: Impact Publications, 1995.
Oldman, Mark, and Hamadeh, Samer. *The Princeton Review: America's Top Internships*. New York: Random House, 1996.
Oldman, Mark, and Hamadeh, Samer. *The Princeton Review: The Internship Bible*. New York: Random House, 1996.
Peterson's. *Internships 1997*. Princeton, N.J.: Peterson's, 1996.

Once you know which companies you want to contact for a possible internship, there are several practical steps you need to take, as follows:

• *Find the right person.* When calling a firm, the person to speak with is the personnel director in the human resources department. This person will know whether the company hires interns and any other details that you might want to know.

• *Get the right information.* Find out what the deadlines are for applying for the internship, whether an in-person or phone interview will be necessary, what the internship responsibilities are, whether the sponsor would be willing to help you get college credit by filling out college paperwork, how long the internship will last, and whether the position pays any salary or stipend.

• *Follow up in writing.* Whatever the deadline for the internship is, be sure to get a resume and cover letter there in time. Seven to ten days after mailing the material, call to make sure it was received. Ask when you can expect to hear from the company next.

• *Never leave a message on the person's voice mail.* If you think that person is going to call you back and add more responsibilities to an already busy day, think again. If you get the voice mail, hang up and call back later. If you get a person and it isn't the person who knows about internships, ask when the person who does know about internships will be available, and call back then. Remember, sound professional.

• *Call early.* When calling someone from whom you want something, try them early in the morning before he or she gets too busy. There's nothing wrong with calling an office at 7:30 A.M.; it's not as if you're going to wake someone up who's already at work!

• *Develop an opening fifteen-second pitch.* Explain who you are, where you're from, and, if you've spoken with the person before, remind her when. It should sound something like this: "Hello, Mr. Smith, this is Dan Johnson from the State College. We spoke three weeks ago about the internship in your sales office. . . ." Once the person on the other end recognizes you, then ask, "Is this a good time to talk?" If she says yes, proceed with your call. If the response is no, ask when a call back would be convenient, and set an exact time. Then say your thank-yous and good-byes, and hang up.

DON'T WORRY! THIS WILL LOOK GOOD ON YOUR RESUME!

CHAPTER 7

Interviewing for an Internship

OK, so you do everything right in your internship search. You find the companies that you want to intern with. You get the right person on the phone, get the info you need, and send him all the materials he needs. Then you're called for an interview. What do you do?

Apart from being well dressed and prompt, most important, be prepared for anything. You should be ready to talk with a potential sponsor for as long as that person allows the conversation to continue. To be ready for the most likely contingencies, pay heed to the following do's and don'ts. They may mean the difference between success and failure.

- If asked about your strongest subjects in school—
  Do: Consider what skills the company needs to fill, and match those, as best you can, with your strongest subjects.
  Don't: List your weakest subjects for them.
- If asked what chores bore you the most—
  Do: Talk about the energetic type of person you are.
  Don't: Lie and pretend nothing bores you.
- If asked about your greatest strengths—
  Do: Talk about your volunteer work and hobbies, and what talents these bring out in you.
  Don't: List your weaknesses in the process of answering the question.

- If asked about the last three books you have read—
  Do: Talk about how one of the books you read pertains to you personally and to the position you're interviewing for.
  Don't: Go into an interview without having three books in mind.
- If asked what you like to do in your spare time—
  Do: Describe what you do, and say it enthusiastically.
  Don't: Downplay your activity, however mundane.
- If asked what you expect to get paid—
  Do: Say you know it is unusual for interns to be paid, but that if a salary does come with the internship, it should be in the general range of what an entry-level employee would make.
  Don't: Get nervous. If someone's willing to pay you, that's a good thing.
- If asked to tell something about yourself—
  Do: Keep it simple and focused on something you know, like school or hobbies.
  Don't: Ramble on about an aspect of your life that might be considered juvenile.
- If asked whether you've worked in an area before, and you haven't—
  Do: Say specifically what you have done elsewhere that might be applicable.
  Don't: Invent something; you're bound to get caught.
- If asked what you can offer a company—
  Do: Accentuate your strengths, such as your intelligence and drive.
  Don't: Undersell yourself by saying, "I'm only a student. I don't know much yet."
- If asked where you expect to be in five years—
  Do: Show ambition and enthusiasm by aiming high.
  Don't: Say that by then you'll be doing the interviewer's job; it might scare someone with a poor sense of humor.
- If asked why you want to work for a specific company—
  Do: Talk about which attributes and values of the company match your own standards.
  Don't: Say you have little or no idea.

Remember, even though you might be grilled with questions by the potential employer, there really are, basically, only three questions on his mind:

1. Can you handle the responsibility?
2. Will you fit in with the other workers?
3. Once on board, will you do the job well?

Any questions that you answer during the interview should be geared toward responding to these three questions.

Keep in mind that the above advice is sound in situations where the interviewer has some experience in interviewing. But, unfortunately, that isn't always the case. In some of your travels, you might happen upon an interviewer who doesn't really know what he is doing. This is a dangerous situation, because this interviewer will not get a correct sense of who you are. The potential employer may walk away from the interview thinking you're not serious enough about working for him when, in fact, it's that person who hasn't a clue, and you wind up without an internship.

If this is the case, you'll get a sense early on that the interviewer is somewhat unfocused. When this happens, you must make your own opportunities to toot your own horn. Here are some guidelines that can still help you make a positive impact when things seem a little off:

- Stick with the objectives that you laid out for yourself before the meeting began. Don't let the interviewer's bewilderment throw you off.
- Look for opportunities where you can stress your positives and still make it seem as though the interviewer is in control of the situation.
- Don't let on that the interview is going poorly. But if it really is going just horribly, you can stop this interview and ask to be seen at another time or by someone else.

Usually when the interview is coming to a close, the interviewer will ask if you have any questions. It's important to ask them; it shows that you are interested in the job. Here are some questions that not only work well but are important for you to have answered:

- How long do your internships run? (semester, year, open-ended)
- How long is the work day, considering that I am still responsible for attending certain classes?
- On which holidays is the office closed?
- Is the building open on the weekends, just in case I have some work to complete?

Even if you don't get the internship, the interview is not a failure if you got something out of the experience. For example, you may learn about another internship elsewhere. Also, if you're not accustomed to interviewing, this experience offered you a chance to practice this skill.

One must—at the end of an interview—sum up what has transpired. The interviewer will often say something reassuring, like, "I'm very impressed with your credentials. You'll hear from us soon." If you don't get a comment like that, try to ascertain where

things stand. You might say something like, "I would very much like to intern here, Mr. Smith. What do you think my chances are for securing this position?"

Whether or not you get the job, always do the following as you're about to leave the interview:

- Thank the interviewer for taking the time to talk with you.
- Ask if there is any additional information you could provide that would instill a better sense of who you are and what you could do for the company.
- Let the interviewer know that you are interested in working for him or her.
- Remind the interviewer that you are a responsible person.

In addition, follow up the interview with a letter. The contents of the letter should include another thank-you for the interviewer's time, a reminder of your interest in the internship, and a restatement of your reasons why you should be hired.

CHAPTER 8

Networking: Your Life's Lost Without It

This is perhaps the most important chapter in this book. Chances are that if you "get it together by 30," you will have done so because of networking. You must master the technique.

Some reports say that at least 80 percent of all jobs in the full-time sector are secured through someone knowing someone else. It shouldn't be a surprise that the cynical real world axiom "It's not what you know, but who you know" is the main determinator of success.

If you're a shy person, networking will be difficult. If you're outgoing, it will be easy. But just like the politician who always runs for office as though she's one vote behind, no matter what your personality, you must continue to network every day as though the next person you meet can change your life—for the better.

On my desk, I keep two Rolodexes, one for the first half of the alphabet, the other for the second—that's how many business cards I've amassed over the years. When I started working after college, my boss sent me to a luncheon with these explicit instructions: Meet as many people as possible, and get a business card from each one. I came back with five or six, and that's how I started my Rolodex.

The significance of growing your Rolodex is that it gives you power in the marketplace. Soon you become known as a person who knows everyone—and you are therefore quite valuable to all the people in your sphere. People will want you because you bring not only your own variety of talents but also a wealth of contacts who can enhance their business.

Invariably, getting to know as many people as possible will give you the ability to refer one person in your network to another person. And the people you have helped will then owe you something for your assistance. Months or years later, when you want something from them, they will usually reciprocate. You'll never know what that something will be; it could be as big as a new job for yourself, or something as ordinary as the name of a good dentist.

Networking is more than just getting to know people; it's about becoming a friend and helping people, with the tacit expectation that you may or may not ever ask them to return the favor—but, in any case, they owe you their loyalty.

—Richard Thau

How do you begin to network? According to experts Sophie Oberstein and Amanda Rose, you first have to know what it is you want to gain from the people whom you are going to talk to. Put simply, you have to have a rehearsed statement about what you are looking for. That way, when someone asks what they can do for you or what kind of work you are looking for, you won't be caught off guard, and your answer will be polished and professional.

One way to start is to memorize the career objective listed on your resume. It should be no longer than a sentence, and basically should be the answer to the question you've been hearing since you were five years old: "What do you want to do when you're grown up?" Until now, it didn't matter. Now it does.

Once you have your goal statement prepared, start telling it to everyone you know. Begin with family and friends. Even if they appear to have no connection at all to your prepared goal, you never know if they might end up helping you. And if all they need to remember is one sentence, then they can get the message out easily to their friends and relatives. A complicated message is like having no message at all.

One of the first things I did after graduating from college was make my own business card. At the time, I already knew that I wanted to find work as a freelance cartoonist, so I figured it would be a pretty good idea to create something I could hand out that would at least tell people I take myself pretty seriously.

Most printers won't print a quantity of less than 500 cards, and frankly it took me years to hand them all out. Also, my initial cost was probably about $60 (most cards are much cheaper, but I used several colors and graphics to display my work), which was a lot for me right after school. Out of those 500 cards, I would say that around 5 directly led me to a job of some sort. Just five? Over the years, those five cards have earned me tens of thousands of dollars. Not bad for a $60 investment.

Since making my own cards for the first time, I've recommended this to everyone. Even if you are still a student, even if you don't have a job or a job title, or even if you only want to print out yur name and phone number, having your own business card not only encourages people to take you seriously, but it's the most convenient way I know to meet people. Say you meet someone you like (and I don't necessarily mean professionally) at a party, a card comes over so much better than fumbling around for a matchbook or napkin to write on. Later on, people are far less likely to reach into their pockets and blow their noses on a business card.

—Nick Bruel

From an actual networking meeting you can obtain not only solid job leads but also names of individuals in the field you're looking to enter, or information about the emerging issues in a field that you can stockpile. Armed with the latter, when you do get to the interview of your dreams, you will sound intelligent about the industry.

People like to talk about their own experiences, particularly their own successes. Ways to start a conversation with someone in a field you want to enter are:

"I'd like to know how you've been successful in this field."
"I'm going to take some classes to help me get up to speed in this area. What would you say are the best classes to take to prepare for a job in your field?"
"I've been reading about this trend in your field in the professional association journals. Do you think that the trend is playing out the way that they report it in the news?"
"Can you tell me what a typical day on the job is like for you? I'm interested in going into this field but don't have a sense of what you do on a day-to-day basis."

After a networking meeting, don't forget to send a thank-you note. And, having done that, remain unforgettable to the contact you met. To do this, Oberstein and Rose suggest sending newspaper articles that might have been mentioned during the meeting. Also, once you've met with someone a source recommended, call, write, or e-mail your source and let that person know how things went. Basically, send things that demonstrate that your follow-up skills are fast and effective.

Also, don't underestimate how you might actually end up helping the person who was supposed to help you. Maybe you'll end up informing him about an upcoming trend, conference, or event. Even if it isn't clear how you might help this person in the foreseeable future, you might end up doing so months or years from now.

If your contact appears to be of little use, then ask the $64,000 question that might just provoke a valuable response: "If you were in my shoes, what would you do? Who would you talk to?" Switching places often gets people to see things your way, including how much help you really need. That question might make a big difference, so don't be afraid to ask it. Remember: The dumbest question is the one that's never asked!

Don't forget to do or say something that stands out positively in the other person's mind. An experienced networker with financial resources—someone in his or her thirties or forties, say—might send flowers, invite the contact to lunch, or send a package via an overnight service so that it's noticed. But for a novice like you, try to stand out by your enthusiasm and timely follow-up efforts.

Finally, if a contact or a series of contacts prove worthless, go outside your circle of friends and family. Try meeting people at the laundry, the gym, or at a place of worship.

CHAPTER 9

Temping: Finding the Upsides to This Interim Career Step

You're probably aware that there is a big change going on in the business world today, with temporary workers—or temps as they're commonly called—becoming a regular fixture at offices across America. The reason for this change is economics; hiring a temp to do work is less expensive than hiring a full-time employee because the company does not pay any benefits to the temp, only a salary through the employment agency.

Working as a temp may sound lousy. You change companies often. There's no guarantee of long-term employment and no chance to climb the company ladder. But that's only one side of the story. Temping can actually be a great opportunity if you take advantage of it. Here are several reasons:

- Temps are never interviewed by the company they actually work for. The temp agency—which conducts a single interview when it first signs a temp on—assigns the job to you. Getting work quickly without the pressure of interviewing directly with an employer can really relieve a lot of the stress that accompanies the job search.
- While working on a temp assignment, if you find that you do not like the company or what you are doing there, most temp agencies will transfer you to another assignment. This transfer usually is not looked on by the temp agency as a strike against you unless your asking to be reassigned becomes a habit. Temping allows you to try many different work environments to see which one is right for you.

• Temp agencies will ask you when you sign up with them whether there is any skill in which you have expertise. Those qualifications will determine what job you get. If this type of work is what you are truly interested in, working in a company will only enhance those skills. Having real-life experience will make you a better choice for an internship and might lead to a full-time job.

• Temp agencies are very flexible. If you have time conflicts, the agency representative will find the work that fits your schedule. Usually agencies can make a job fit your needs because they can arrange a deal with the company that you probably couldn't have done by yourself. Temp agencies have leverage you don't have on your own.

• A temp job can often lead to an arrangement where you leave your temp assignment and become a full-fledged employee of a company where you've been temping. But beware: Temp agencies are on the lookout for these types of arrangements (where they lose a paying client). And in the future—when you might need a temp job again—your name could be mud.

CHAPTER 10

Getting Yourself Mentally Prepared for a Full Job Search

There's a lot more to looking for a job than looking for a job. That may not make sense at first blush, but think about it: You have to be mentally prepared for everything that will come at you as you undertake your search, even before you look at your first classified ad or call your first potential job contact.

To get through all the mental muck that prevents you from getting started, or keeps you moving at much too slow a pace, remember the following advice:

• *Be yourself:* When approaching someone you hope will be a potential contact, there is no reason to be nervous. When people are asking you questions about your likes and dislikes, they are not looking for some hidden meaning, they are trying to get to know you. Finding a job doesn't happen only to those who are masters of small talk and can sell water to a drowning man. Doing your homework, thinking through answers to questions you might ask, and preparing questions for the interviewer will allow you to be yourself when the time comes to be interviewed.

• *Understand patience:* There will be moments when you feel that all the work you have been doing is a waste of time. You're entitled to feel like that; most of the preparation you do will end with someone deciding to turn you down.

To remedy this feeling, it usually helps to put your thoughts toward the long haul. Visualize your dream job way down the line. Now see what you can do today to get there. Concern yourself with what you can do today.

Consider, for example, a student who's thinking of becoming a doctor. This person shouldn't be worrying about medical school exams but rather about what subjects to take in college that will better prepare her for those exams. There is a saying that "inch by inch, anything is a cinch." Taking life moment by moment is all we can do, because moments are all we are given at one time.

• *Remember, laughter is the best medicine:* When Ronald Reagan was shot in 1981, he wisecracked his way through the whole ordeal. Upon arriving at the hospital, he told the medical staff, "All in all, I'd rather be in Philadelphia." Then he told his surgeons, "I hope you're all Republicans." Even during a crisis, defusing tensions with humor is extremely effective. It can work wonders during your job search.

• *"Fake it till you make it":* This slogan was made popular by John D. Rockefeller. Even though it sounds like lying, it's actually helpful. It is an affirmation. It's telling yourself that soon you will make it and for now, you are telling people about it in advance of its happening. There's no lie in telling people early on what is going to happen to

you. If you'd asked Madonna, before she became a star, what she was planning to do with her life, she would have told you she was planning to make it big. She wasn't lying, she was just giving you early warning.

• *Don't forget that things have changed:* While you attended college or a trade school, employers saw at you as a student. And, like it or not, in the back of their minds they saw you as a nonemployee. If you erred a few times, they chalked it up to a learning experience. Also, if you had second thoughts about the internship you had chosen, you could usually redirect yourself into a different career field with little or no trouble.

That changed with graduation.

Now you're in a totally different environment. Employers view a prospective employee with many prior career changes as someone who is indecisive and possibly too risky to hire. Isn't it strange? If you've had a host of internship experiences, that's considered great. If you've had a host of different jobs, that's looked upon as bad.

And if you aren't one of the lucky ones to get hired directly from your internship and are still looking for work, you are in for a true challenge. You are now going to be in competition for a particular job with people who might have years of experience and a deeper hands-on knowledge of what a company expects from an employee to ensure the work gets done.

Finally, once you are hired, any problems that you might cause the company could result in your being fired.

In other words, since you've graduated, employers expect more out of you from the start. They are no longer obliged by any internship program to keep you around if they don't see you fitting in with the goals of their corporation. They will no longer lend a sympathetic ear to listen to your scheduling traumas or lack of vacation days. The first year out of school takes graduates by surprise; if they have found a job, they do not get summer off, and whether employed or not, when Labor Day comes around, they watch as younger friends and relatives head back to school.

From this point forward, we will presume you know what type of job you wish to pursue. For those who are undecided, the sections that follow will not apply immediately. But, in either case, the upcoming chapters present a road map of your future—whenever you're ready to take the trip.

CHAPTER 11

Getting Your Resume Over the Toughest Hurdles

Your resume is often a potential employer's first impression of you. Think of the resume as being the paper history of you—reduced to just one page. It is a major ingredient in the process of getting hired and putting your best foot forward early.

And it better be your best foot forward. The typical human resources person takes just a few seconds to peruse a resume. If she does not find anything interesting in that short span, you can consider yourself out of the running for the employment opportunity. By the way, if you think a human resources director, or any other person in charge of hiring, actually reads your resume when it is first received, you are mistaken. When the resume arrives, it is skimmed—at most. The employer is looking for something that strikes him or stands out about you, rather than the experiences you've had in the classroom or even on the job.

If this cursory "scanning" isn't cause enough to worry about getting an interview with the company of your dreams, the number of resumes a typical company receives will surely give you pause. In his book *The Resume Kit*, Richard H. Beatty offers a description of how many resumes pass before an employer's eyes in one year. He states, "In larger companies, it is not uncommon for the corporate employment department to receive as many as 40,000 to 50,000 resumes during the course of an average business year. Some receive considerably more."

These larger companies typically hire 200 to 300 employees each year, averaging two to three interviews per hire. A quick calculation shows that large firms will interview between 400 and 900 employment candidates in meeting these requirements. That's not a lot of interviews, considering that up to 50,000 resumes are received annually. Just think: At this rate, if you mail 100 resumes, only one or two will lead to an interview.

> Believe it or not, I was once granted a job interview not because of the content of my resume but purely because of the way it looked. The interview was for an assistant art director position at a pretty prominent theater company. Actually, my resume is really not that spectacular looking. There are no colors or graphics or wacky fonts. As any resume should be, it is organized conservatively. But this man loved the way it looked. He told me he liked the way I used tab indents and underlining and bold highlights to organize my information. I never thought about it that much until then. But as a designer, he found the fact that my resume was *easy to read* to be a crucial element. In the long run, ensuring that the content of your resume is relevant is extremely important, but also making it legible and good-looking sure can't hurt.
>
> –Nick Bruel

So what can you do to lessen the chances that your resume is tossed in the wastebasket while the scanning process is going on? The best defense is knowledge. If you know what a person is looking for, or not looking for, in a resume, it can help guide you in arranging yours. Read these "Guaranteed Rejection Steps" carefully—and *don't* try them at home!

Resume "Guaranteed Rejection Steps":
Do These And You Don't Stand a Chance!

- Make sure your career objective bears no relation to the job being offered.

- List mediocre grades on your resume.
- Live nowhere near the employer.
- Pick a hard-to-read font for your resume.
- Lay your resume out in a unique format that takes time to decipher.
- Show that you've held lots of unrelated jobs in a short period of time.
- Put your resume on two pages because you think you're very important.

We know some of these "guaranteed rejection steps" are out of your immediate control, like where you live. So don't worry about them. Only fix, or work on, what is under your control. In the real job world there are going to be a lot of factors over which you have no control. But they still have an effect on whether you get a job. Becoming accustomed to these outside factors now will alleviate many headaches in the future.

During my days in journalism I was once asked by the editor of the magazine to find and hire a new associate editor. So I put a classified ad in *The New York Times*, and waited for the mail to pour in. It did.

We received more than 200 resumes in just over a week; some days more than fifty arrived. How do you think I ever figured out whom to interview?

Well, back when I was in college, I'd served on an ad hoc committee to choose a new admissions officer. On the committee was the director of admissions, who explained that the smartest way to begin the evaluation process was for each committee member to look over each resume, and put it in one of three piles: "yes", "maybe," or "no." Then, once everyone had evaluated all the resumes, the ones receiving a "yes" most often would be the ones most likely to get a second look.

So that's what I did for this editor's job, except that I was the only person who evaluated the resumes, so what I chose was final. How I made my choices was simple: I came in on a Saturday and sat on the floor with this massive pile in front of me, and started categorizing each resume. Using the guaranteed rejection steps cited above, I chose the resumes I liked best.

At the end of the day, I had a small "yes" pile, and two pretty large "maybe" and "no" piles. Then I prioritized the "yes" pile in order of desirability. The following Monday I started calling people in for interviews.

–Richard Thau

If you do survive the first skimming of your resume, the employer will then take a second look before calling in people for interviews. In this next pass, the hiring firm is no longer scanning the resume but really reading it as well as the cover letter, and trying to get a feel for who the person is and what talents would be brought to the firm. Meeting these "second pass" qualities usually ensures you an interview with the firm.

Second Pass Qualities That Get You an Interview

- Candidate has the correct number of years of experience and possesses the right level of expertise. This is a matter of luck more than anything else. You can't do much more than make sure you apply for jobs where you know you stand a chance because you meet the employer's most basic criteria.
- Candidate has proven him or herself to have the right management or leadership skills. Be sure the resume outlines your skills accurately; as much as you don't want to oversell yourself, or pad your resume, be sure not to undersell yourself either.
- Candidate shows a solid record of accomplishment. Again, don't be shy about what you've done. Just be honest—and clear.
- Candidate's resume stands up well, relative to the other resumes submitted to the company. Again, part of this is luck. If the other candidates are unusually weak, that helps your chances. But don't bank on this. Most employers are in a buyer's market and can choose among many qualified candidates.

If you do get "the call," rejoice. Your resume has proved you worthy of being considered for employment, which is something deserving of celebration. To help you with the interviewing process, jump to Chapters 17 through 19, and you will find what you need to know to prepare for the interview. To find out where to look to research the company that is interviewing you, go to Chapter 21.

Now let's say, for argument's sake, that you have found the company that possesses the qualities you want (how to determine whether you've found such a company will be discussed in Chapters 19 and 20) and that it also has an opening for a job you happen to be interested in and wish to pursue on the way to a lifelong career. How do you make certain, as the human resources director scans your resume for the first time, that his or her fleeting seconds—and your chances of getting in the door—are not squandered? And how do you better ensure that yours will be the one out of 100 resumes that results in a call for an interview?

It's simple. Have a dynamite resume.

Where do you start? At the beginning. You start at the beginning of your life, and you literally write down everything that you have accomplished, keeping in mind your career objective. If you were a math tutor as a kid, and your career objective is to go into teaching, jot down on that piece of paper—under "teaching experience"—your tutoring job. Nothing is too small for you not to write it down at this moment (you'll obviously remove it later), as you take the very first steps in constructing your resume.

Another very important tip: Although employers want to know your jobs, they need to view your accomplishments even more. Instead of telling them on your resume that you had a tutoring business, tell them that your students' test scores increased by 15 percent.

(You know what we're saying here. Let's assume that as you were building your tutoring business, you found that your students kept referring you to their friends. Soon you were making enough money to put some away for college. Not bad for a 16-year-old. Good work! NOW, WRITE IT DOWN! It will probably spur some other memory of greater relevance to your job search.)

For those of you who have had jobs since owning and operating your tutoring business, think back. What did you do on those jobs that impressed your boss? What were you doing when your supervisor said, "Good job" or "Job well done" to you? Those situations should be on your resume. Suppose, for example, that you worked in a clothing store as a floor salesperson and during that time period sales went up by 10 percent. This job should be listed like so, on your resume:

Salesperson: Increased sales annually by 10% working for ABC Shoes.

What writing down all your accomplishments will do for you is open your mind to experiences and phases that you might have forgotten. Most people, when they begin working on their resumes, have trouble putting down not only the correct information but enough information. A common joke about first-time job seekers is that they could put all their qualifications on the cover of a matchbook. But after undertaking the exercise described here, you can see you have a lot to offer a potential employer.

Another important factor to remember when building a resume is that this piece of paper will be the first impression an employer has

of you. It is a reflection of who you are and what you have accomplished. If it is concise and clearly written to show that you are not only competent but also competitive, you can rest assured that your best foot has been put forward.

So put this book down for awhile and write down your achievements to date.

Do not forget to include awards you have won inside or outside of school. Anything that helps define who you are will bring merit to your resume and give the employer a greater sense of who you are.

CHAPTER 12

The Different Types of Resumes

Now that you have listed your accomplishments and awards, how do you place them on the resume? And, more importantly, what do you leave in or leave out of your resume? What you do with your information will depend greatly on what type of job you are going after—and what type of resume you wish to send out.

There are three basic types of resumes. Each one is tailored for a specific use based on what you wish your resume to accomplish. The three types of resumes are: (1) chronological, (2) functional, and (3) targeted.

The Chronological Resume

The most common type of resume is the chronological, and it will typically elicit the most interviews, simply because it is the style that employers are accustomed to when scanning for potential hires. Your accomplishments on such a resume are listed in reverse chronological order. Also, these accomplishments are broken down into subject segments (Experience, Education, and so on).

For example, suppose you had a job in a shoe store as a salesperson for two years. And before this job you also worked as a salesman in a pet shop. These jobs would be under your "Experience" segment and your most recent job would be listed first. The Experience section of your resume would look like this:

```
EXPERIENCE

1993-1996    Salesman, ABC Shoes: Increased sales annually by 10%.

1989-1992    Assistant Salesman, DEF Pet Store: Assisted in
increasing the store's gross sales of dog-walking supplies
by 25% over the course of employment.
```

Most employers look for this type of format in the resumes they receive. But, if you aren't sure when to use this format, here are the instances when the chronological resume is a must:

• When your work history shows development (meaning advances) in your career. As the above example illustrates, for the years 1989 to 1992, this person was an assistant salesperson. And from the years 1993 to 1996, this person was a full salesperson. This development in career is important for an employer to notice, and the chronological resume highlights this aspect more successfully than the other resume types.

• When the person you have most recently worked for, or are currently working with, is well-known within the industry. There is an old saying that "Proximity to power is power." If you have been working for a prestigious employer, one that a potential employer would be impressed with, allow that human resources director to see it first. That bit of information alone might get you an interview.

• When the company you are sending the resume to expects it to be formatted in chronological order. Most large companies do anticipate reviewing resumes that are set up this way.

The Functional Resume

The functional resume is used when you want to show off your achievements. These accomplishments could reflect your school days or extracurricular activities; they do not have to reflect only the work arena. The main purpose of this style of resume is to show the employer what you are capable of, not just what you have done in the past.

An example of a portion of this type of resume follows:

<u>Management:</u> Have overseen and delegated duties to 25 people. Have been a troubleshooter for a sales firm.

<u>Computer:</u> Have knowledge of Microsoft Word and many database programs.

It is most advantageous to use the functional resume in the following scenarios:

- When the capabilities you wish to emphasize have not been exercised during recent employment. If you have been away from a certain skill for any length of time, an employer may shy away from choosing you to be interviewed. Let prospective employers call you in, then tell them when you last performed those duties.
- When you are just starting out and do not have much work-related experience. Normally, in such situations you would want to show off accomplishments that occurred while you were in school. You would choose, of course, those positive aspects that would enhance your chances of getting the interview.
- When you have had many jobs in no one specific area. Unconnected jobs, such as freelancing or temp work, might look like a negative attribute in employers' eyes. They like to see that their potential employees have had long-term relationships with their old employers. Jumping around from job to job could prevent you from getting the interview. Using the functional resume will enhance your positives and keep what the employer might view as negative in check until the interview. But by that time you'll already have won them over with your other winning attributes.
- When you are changing careers. Some potential employers view people who change careers as indecisive and who therefore might change their minds again. It's a very conservative view, but that is usually how the corporate world operates. Corporate America is often afraid to train someone who has a history of changing his mind because, if the employee repeats this pattern, the employer has wasted money on training that person and is forced to begin the process of hiring and training all over again.

The Targeted Resume

The targeted resume is appropriate when you are zeroing in on a specific job. You may create several targeted resumes for yourself, depending on how many jobs you wish to pursue. One item to keep in mind when sending out the targeted resume: Make sure the job you are targeting is available with the employer to whom you are sending it. It may sound ridiculous, but you'd be surprised how many people use this form of resume when the job they are targeting isn't even available.

A targeted resume usually begins with your job objective. This statement is usually concise, and it allows no doubt to enter the employer's mind as to what type of job you're after. Once the job objective is stated, you then prove that you possess the capabilities to do the job. This portion of the resume could be formatted along the lines of the chronological resume or the functional resume. Decide which style to use on the basis of which resume will put you in the best light. To figure that out, follow the rules of thumb that accompany the description of each resume.

Examples of the targeted resume, used in conjunction with a chronological format and a functional one, are as follows:

Targeted Resume Using the Chronological Format

Objective:

To secure a position in your company's computer department as an MIS professional.

Experience:

1994-present MIS Assistant, ABC Company: Assisted in the development of the company's home pages, which are now marketed worldwide.

1992-1994 Computer Programmer, Microsoft: Served as support to Bill Gates at Microsoft while developing Windows '95.

Targeted Resume Using the Functional Format

Objective:

To secure a position in your company's computer department as an MIS professional.

Education:

Graduated Summa Cum Laude from Slippery Rock University, majoring in computers.

Awards:

Was voted, for the year 1995, by the Institute for Certification of Computer Professionals (ICCP), a national professional computer organization, most likely to succeed in my field.

The message you are trying to convey to the prospective employer with the targeted resume is that you are after one job—and one job only. Also, you have been working toward this goal for some time and feel you are ready to take that next step in the path of your life-long career choice. If you don't have a strong desire for one such job, the targeted resume is very likely *not* the one for you. The best circumstances to use a resume such as this one are:

- When you are clear on your next move.
- When you want to apply to one specific field or a number of specific fields. (Of course, you need to create one resume for each field you decide to enter.)

Which of the Three Resume Styles Should You Use?

As a general rule of thumb, when deciding which resume format to create, keep in mind what attributes you possess and which style would best show them off. This is crucial. Imagine yourself as an employer scanning *your* resume. What turns you off? What turns you on? And, more importantly, what aspect of your resume would cause you to be curious enough to call you in for an interview? That's the bottom line to the question as to which type of resume to use: Which one will put you in the best light and be most likely to secure you an interview?

CHAPTER 13

Your Resume Format

Now that you have all your information about yourself, and know which resume style would be the most advantageous, what do you put where? Also, and more importantly, which items of your life would be best suited for the resume, and which ones should you leave out?

Well, the answer to these questions is, it depends. Just as with deciding which resume style is right for you, so it goes for what items to include in your resume. If it helps you get the job, put it on; if not, leave it off.

This rule of thumb is not specific, and some of you might wish to have a less general, more direct guide on how to construct your resume. To help you decide what headings to put on your resume and what should follow them, follow Jeffrey Allen's advice in *The Resume Makeover* and discover what your resume's format should comprise. Please keep in mind, while you read this section, what type of resume style best fits your qualifications and how these tips can be meshed to fit with the resume type you have chosen.

The first tip to keep in mind: Never title your resume "Resume." The employer looking over your qualifications will understand what he or she is viewing!

Segments to Your Resume

• *Identification:* No matter what style resume you have chosen, this item should be at the top. Whether the ID goes on the top center or on the top left is up to you. One item to remember about your heading: Never place it on the top right, since it might confuse the resume with a cover letter.

Your identification should include your name, address, telephone number, and possibly your e-mail address and Social Security number. Letting readers know that you have a Social Security number lessens the possibility of someone thinking you are an illegal alien or a person who is on a limited visa.

• *Related Work Experience:* This section is where you must shine. Employers who read your resume will be scrutinizing this area. Above all, this section must be compatible with the job that is open within the company for you to be considered for an interview. If you had an internship that is related to the job you are looking for, put it here. If you have any outstanding achievements that could sway an employer to bringing you in, put them here. Employers will not consider you for an interview unless you tell them about your practical knowledge and experience. Remember, for this section, allow the most room to be used for what you are doing currently.

• *Education:* Where this item appears on your resume should depend on how recently you graduated from the last school you attended. If you went to college or a trade school, there is no reason for you to include where you attended high school. The employer will assume you finished one level if you have completed the next highest level.

Placing your grade point average (GPA) on your resume is advised only if you had an outstanding GPA. By the term "outstanding" let's be generous and mean that you had no lower than a 3.3 GPA out of a possible 4.0. Of course, what really will determine whether you should put your grade point average on your resume is what job you are seeking. Some employers are not as concerned about grades as others. What most employers like to see is that you graduated from the last level of school that you attended. This shows them that you finish what you start, an essential quality any employer wants in abundance.

• *Volunteer Work:* This experience can be invaluable, if what you did as a volunteer is similar to the job you are now seeking. Most volunteer programs do work like a "normal" business, where everyday duties are required. If you fulfilled one of those jobs, putting those tasks down on your resume will show that you are no stranger to the workplace, a quality employers like to see in their new recruits.

• *Professional Organizations:* Belonging to such enterprises shows the level of commitment you have to the career you have chosen, and employers like seeing this quality in employees. Membership in such groups can sometimes balance out a poor or questionable grade point average or thin work experience. This section is where you may want to list any awards you have received as well.

• *Special Abilities and Skills:* Items from this category are usually listed to enhance your chances of securing the interview. This is the area where you show yourself to be well-rounded, still keeping in mind your objective of finding the job of your dreams. An example of an attribute that might be listed here would be speaking, reading, or writing different languages.

• *General Business Skills:* If you are planning to have a targeted or functional resume, here is where you would want to communicate to the employer that you know your way around an office. In this section you would inform the human resources director that you know a number of word processing programs and are familiar with the Internet (if you are). Similar advice applies to job skills in other fields, such as health care, industrial management, or food service.

• *Military Background:* Being a member of the armed services, no matter what branch, is an honor. It's hard to imagine any employer seeing your service to your country as reason to preclude you from an interview, but some might. Some employers will see your service, the rank you held, and wonder what it means in civilian experience. If you spent a long time in the service, they really might not know how to judge your work experience. To counteract this issue, Allen suggests listing the civilian equivalent of your military duties side by side. An example would be as follows:

Military Service	***Civilian Equivalent***
Supply Sergeant	Warehouse Foreman
Motor Pool Captain	Traffic Manager
Naval Communication Officer	Telecommunications Manager

If you spent only a few years in the service, all you really need to account for is the time you were there, so your resume doesn't have any time gaps in it. Be sure to state that you were honorably discharged (assuming you were).

• *Personal Information:* Most employers would probably be surprised to see this information on your resume. Personal facts, in recent years, have been a source of controversy. Companies no longer have a right to ask you questions unrelated to work. But if you feel there is some attribute in your personal life that could help you get a job, by all means, put that fact on your resume. A word of caution, though. Items like your sex, age, race, marital status, or religion should never be on a resume. Also, never put that you are in excellent health, because employers usually assume this from all their potential employees.

• *References:* It is unprofessional to include people's names on your resume. Instead, write, "References available upon request." Putting this sentence down will remind you to warn your references that a potential employer might be calling them. You can coach them on what you wish them to say, specifically any comments that you feel the employer would like to hear about you. Also, you must have a separate reference list ready for anyone who requests one. Employers who ask for them are almost certainly going to check them. Don't look foolish; make sure the names are spelled correctly and the titles, addresses, and phone numbers are updated.

Food for Thought

If you lack the work experience or training necessary for the job you desire, you may want to lead off with other special accomplishments that you have had, such as making the dean's list in college or winning some award that denotes your outstanding character. If none of these attributes define you, think back; there is sure to be something of merit that you have achieved.

Also, if you have experienced periods in your life where you did not have a job or weren't in school, and you've decided to use the chronological resume, there is one piece of advice you must, must take: Don't lie. If you didn't do anything of importance toward your career goal for a few years, just leave that period of your life out of your resume.

My first job out of college was with a company that verified information on resumes and job applications to ensure that they were accurate. Companies like this are becoming increasingly prevalent, so beware: Don't fudge your resume.

I caught a couple of people in their own untruths and they were likely fired or severely reprimanded.

One person said he'd graduated from Iona University, and I became immediately suspicious. Iona is a college, not a university, and anyone attending Iona would know that. I called the registrar's office at Iona College just to make sure, and they had no record of him.

Another person listed four jobs, each lasting two years, that spanned a total of eight years. When I checked each one out, something strange happened. The person had indeed worked at each job, but only for one year each time. So it clearly seemed that either he had a very poor memory, or he was trying to cover up something by doubling the length of his employment history.

Finally, don't get funny or overly euphemistic with your resume. One person who had worked at a gas station said he'd been a "fuel transfer technician"; in other words, he pumped gas. I had a good laugh, but I have no idea how the prospective employer reacted.

–Richard Thau

Another tip: Don't send a picture of yourself with your resume. Employers don't know what to do with them. They feel awkward when this situation arises and may not call you in for that very reason. Besides, on the first pass, the employer spends only a few seconds scanning your resume. You don't want to make him or her uneasy and forget to look at your resume before moving on to the next candidate.

To make sure the employer reads your resume correctly and does not get confused by all your information, you may want to begin each new entry that falls under your headings with a bullet. Now, I don't mean the silver kind that the Lone Ranger carries. I mean the type that is found on your keyboard or within your word processing program. A bullet is this: •. Having this symbol (or some other visual indicator such as boldface or underlined type) start each segment allows the employer to know when a new element of your resume begins.

SAMPLE RESUME:

DICK Q. PUBLIC
123 Main Street
Anytown, USA 12345
(212) 555-2001

EXPERIENCE

Innovate or Emigrate (June 1993 to present)
817 State Street - 9th Floor, Newark, NJ 06723

Executive Director & Cofounder
Lead the national organization as its chief administrator and executive. Undertake all short- and long-range planning, interface with regional chapters across the United States, devise annual and project budgets, coordinate press conferences with members of Congress and leading political figures, testify before Congressional committees regarding issues, write opinion pieces for *The New York Times*, *Newsday* and *Christian Science Monitor*, respond to journalists' queries, appear on dozens of national and local radio and TV shows, fulfill all legal and accounting obligations, recruit new members, and help raise nearly $500,000 to operate the nonprofit group from its inception to its maturity.

Gaseous Fumes News (Oct. 1989 to June 1993)
49 East 21 Street, New York, NY 10010

Senior Editor (Sept. 1990 to June 1993)
Associate Editor (Oct. 1989 to Sept. 1990)

Write between five and eight stories each week pertaining to all aspects of the gas industry. Focus on fume containment,the purchase or sale of gas properties, the launch of new companies and the restructuring of others, legal or political issues, and miscellaneous controversial subjects.

Guide other staffers with their magazine work, including their choice of stories and writing angles. Find, hire, and supervise student interns. Represent the magazine at industry receptions, cover monthly lunch meetings of trade organizations, speak at *Gaseous Fumes News* seminars, and travel across the United States, to report on annual magazine industry conferences.

Conceive and execute a charity program that regularly donates the New York bureau's surplus magazines to hospital waiting rooms. Organize and sponsor a magazine T-shirt contest that donates dozens of post-contest entries to New York-based charities.

EDUCATION

Half Heart College, Half Heart, PA: B.A., History (May 1987)
Honors: Phi Beta Kappa; History Department Honors
Extracurriculars: Chairman of Heart Council (Feb. 1986 to Feb. 1987)
Columnist for *Half Heart News* (1984)
Campus Tour Guide (Sept. 1984 to May 1987)

COMPUTER SKILLS
Microsoft Word, WordPerfect, FileMaker Pro, Internet Search Engines

REFERENCES
Available Upon Request

CHAPTER 14

How to Finesse the Cover Letter

Once you have completed your resume and have found the companies that you wish to target, you are nearly ready to make contact. The only item missing from the employer's first impression of you is a cover letter.

There is a universal question about cover letters: Do employers really read them or do they get thrown in the trash? The answer: Always presume that they get read. After all of the good schoolwork you've done, the years of education you have endured, don't blow it away by focusing all your attention on the resume and neglecting the cover letter. If you write a poor one, it may very well be held against you. If your resume is one among several belonging to equally qualified candidates, the cover letter could decide your fate—in either direction.

Basically, a cover letter is your way of making a first impression. It's used to whet the appetite of the employer so he or she will read your resume and want to call you in. A cover letter should never run more than three paragraphs and should never cover more than two-thirds of the page. Think of it this way: If the human resources director is spending, say, twenty seconds on you on the first pass, perhaps seven of those twenty seconds will be used to skim your cover letter. You must make it quick and interesting.

The cover letter format should include:

• Your name and address: This information may be typed in the top right corner or included on personal letterhead.

• Date: Should be about an inch and a half down the page, flush left.

Note: Skip one space before beginning the next section.

• Employer's identification: It is always better to have the person's name to whom you are sending the resume; it's more professional. But sometimes only a title is available and you'll have to make do with it. The address should appear identical to the way it will be on the envelope. The standard format is the person's name, title, company name, address. Don't include the phone number.

Note: Skip one space before beginning the next section.

• Job opening: Here is where you would type "Re:" followed by the job for which you are applying. Remember, if the job opening was found in the want ads, take their description of the job and retype it here. Don't make up your own title for the job if one is given; it might be misconstrued as for the wrong job opening and you might be mistakenly disqualified before you are even considered.

Note: Skip one space before beginning the next section.

• Salutation: Always address the person using his or her surname and the proper title before it. A word of advice: If the person to whom you are writing is a woman, and you do not know her marital status, address the letter to "Ms. ________," not "Miss ________" or "Mrs.__________." The last thing you want to do is give offense to someone before he or she ever even reads your letter. "Ms." is now considered as neutral to women as "Mr." is to men. If you cannot tell the person's gender from the name, just repeat the whole name: "Dear Terry Smith."

Note: Skip one space before beginning the next section.

• The body of the letter: Remember to compose only three paragraphs (at most) and keep them all short. Your mission within these lines is to complement your resume, not repeat it. (Keep in mind, insert only one space between paragraphs.)

• The first paragraph: The first sentence needs to have punch, something that will catch the reader's attention and make him or her want to read on. The most obvious one is the name of the person who referred you (if you were actually referred). In that case, the letter should begin with "[fill in name] suggested that I contact you." If you were referred, don't be shy about it; it establishes an instant bond between you and the reader and helps ensure that the letter gets past the secretary who opens the mail.

If you don't have a referral, then you have to get creative, particularly if you're responding to a classified ad. Talk about how the ad, or something particular in it, piqued your interest. Take your time writing it. It is difficult. But do everything you can not to be boring.

• The second paragraph: In this section you want to really sell yourself. Here you link your accomplishments to the qualifications that the prospective employer wants to fill. Also, if the employer has asked for your salary requirement, be sure to put it here, but in range form ("from $22,000 to $25,000") to show that you are flexible.

• The third paragraph: A boilerplate ending is fine here. You should end with something like this: "Thank you for taking the time to peruse my resume. I eagerly anticipate hearing from you soon. I will follow up with a call next week, but if you need to reach me in the meantime, my telephone number is . . ."

Note: Skip one space before beginning the next section.

• Closing salutation: Here is where you sign off. Be safe. Write "Sincerely,"

Note: Skip four spaces before beginning the next section.

• Your name: Write your name as it appears on your resume.

Note: Skip two spaces before beginning the next section.

• Indication of an enclosure: Writing "encl." flush left on the page's margin will tell the employer that another item has accompanied your cover letter, which happens to be your resume.

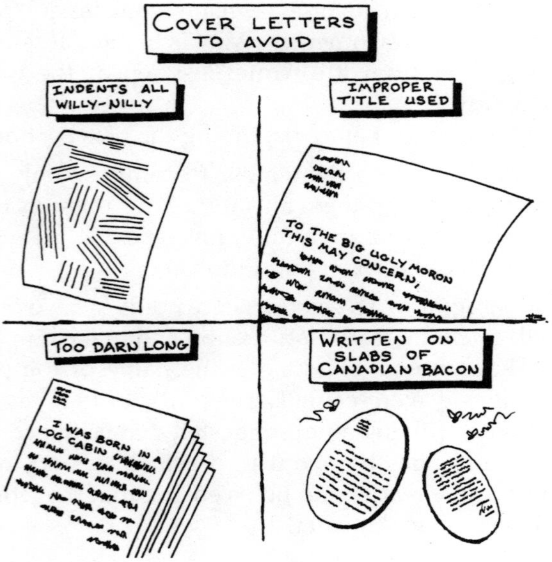

Some final pointers:

- The cleanest-looking cover letters have all lines beginning flush left.
- The text within paragraphs should be single-spaced.
- Personal letterhead might help you look professional. But if you don't have it or can't afford it, be sure your self-created letterhead is neat and organized.
- Do not ask a prospective employer to contact you via e-mail. The technology is still not consistent enough that you want your job prospects to hinge on it.

Sample Cover Letter

July 1, 1997

Mr. John Stein
Human Resources Director
Just Shoelaces, Inc.
110 Nike Lane, Suite 937
Chicago, IL 60656

Re: Salesperson position advertised in the *Chicago Tribune*

Dear Mr. Stein:

After winning my firm's outstanding salesperson award for the third consecutive year, I believe I would make a good candidate for the job opening you have listed in last Sunday's *Chicago Tribune.*

Selling has always been a passion of mine, and I have always met with success while working in the field. Before joining my most recent employer, I increased my last employer's sales production by more than 25 percent annually. My campaigns were so successful that I was named "employee of the month" eight times in 18 months. Now I am seeking a different type of selling challenge.

Thank you for taking the time to peruse my resume. I eagerly anticipate hearing from you soon. I will follow up with a call next week, but if you need to reach me in the meantime, my telephone number is 312-555-1212.

Sincerely,

Mike Johnston

encl.

CHAPTER 15

Building Your Career Electronically

The Internet and online services have moved from being the object of interesting party chatter and the realm of geeks and propellerheads to the everyday mainstream of our culture.

These days a person with some spare time, a computer, a modem, and an account with an online service such as America Online, Prodigy, or CompuServe or an Internet service provider can shop online, date online, buy stocks online, look for a house online, get a recipe online, show vacation photos online (though this might risk some reprisals), and argue politics with people of like or different mind halfway across the planet.

According to Jupiter Communications, a New York–based new media research firm that tracks the growth of the Internet and online services, more than 35 million households are expected to connect to cyberspace via their modems by the year 2000. That's more than one out of every three American homes.

Because of the smart work of information entrepreneurs, just about anything you can think of can be done across the vast networks of computers that now crisscross the globe, including much of what is in this book: looking for a job, getting advice about how to get the one you want, keep the one you have, get a start working for yourself, or generally how to plot and plan your career.

Even if you aren't "net-savvy," you can make good use of the wonderful resources detailed in the following pages, and the great thing is that they are available twenty-four hours a day, seven days a week, and are updated often, meaning the information is fresh and useful. If you don't have a personal computer, and many of us don't (especially if we are just starting out), you can either get a friend to help you or try your local library, university or an Internet cafe, if your town has one. The great thing about the techno-revolution sweeping America and the rest of the planet is that there is now probably a computer near you.

■ Using an Online Service

Before the World Wide Web and the rest of the Internet took the world by storm in 1995, the most widely used way to get information, be entertained, and socialize from your computer was the online services. An outgrowth of the computer bulletin boards that cropped up around the country in the 1980s, online services have grown fast over the past two years, though the advent of the Web as a friendly (and often cheaper) place to find information has forced these services to open up to the Internet.

The main online services covered here are America Online and CompuServe. Between them, they currently have more than 10 million subscribers, or people who pay a fee to use the services. If you haven't tried one before, they can be a great way to get to know other people, get access to newspapers and magazines, get an e-mail address (an increasingly important symbol in today's information marketplace), and, of course, find great information about how to build your career.

Just a note before we go further: Online job searches are not a black hole. We have actual firsthand experience with them, having made contact and actually been invited for interviews based on contacts made over these very services. Many of today's top employers are looking for the sort of technically able people who use online resources and show the initiative to look for opportunities. Good jobs and great contacts can be at the other end of an online connection.

Later in this chapter, we will look at placing your resume in cyberspace, but for now, let's take a look at just some of what's available online to help you get your career going and keep it going.

For those with access to an online service, there are a number of resources at your fingertips that can get you started on the road to career information. Two major online services—America Online and CompuServe—house extensive job information and provide both postings of positions wanted and positions to be filled.

To navigate online, you'll need to use *keywords*: terms that may be entered in each service's quick area locator utility. America Online uses "keyword" and CompuServe uses the term "Go." Check with each service for more instructions on how to get quickly from point to point within the service.

America Online

As the largest online service (it had over 8 million members at the time of this writing), America Online is a fantastic resource for those wanting to speed their career along. From articles on employment to searchable databases of jobs, there isn't much you can't find here.

The focal point of job information on America Online is the Career Center (keywords: Career, Center). Moderated by James Gonyea, one of the godfathers of electronic job resources, the Career Center is a great place to start your information search or come back weekly or monthly to sharpen your skills or check for job openings. Checking with this area frequently is like having your own personal career counselor on retainer.

The Career Center houses several types of information, including searchable databases of jobs posted by employers nationwide and catalogs of career information—for example, articles by top career advice specialists, sample resumes, and sample cover letters. Below are some of the highlights:

- *Career Articles:* These change often, as do these services overall. Typical fare includes an article about planting good keywords throughout your online resume to make it more useful when potential employers go searching Internet resume databases, or updated information on new procedures for applying for federal jobs.

• *Federal Government Employment Opportunities:* Interested in working for the government? Here's the place. This area gives you tips about securing a government job (it can be trickier than you think), whom you should contact, what options are available to you as a job hunter, what skills you will need, an outline of government departments, and—most important of all—a list of federal government positions that need to be filled.

• *Talent Bank:* These features are a growing trend in electronic job bulletin boards: a place where you can either post your resume or search for those of others. They are generally searchable by key terms, so think carefully about how your resume is worded (see section on electronic resumes above).

• *Resume Templates:* Your cousin says it should look one way, your school counselor another. Who's right? Take a browse through the Career Center's resume templates and see what style of resume suits you and your career goals best.

• *Cover Letter Templates:* We can't say it enough times. Cover letters are your future employer's introduction to you. You don't want to get this one wrong, so look into the cover letter template library and see which one matches the occasion.

• *Help Wanted-USA:* Still a great service even in a world of searchable databases, Help Wanted-USA is a great way to plow through hundreds of job listings to find what you want. Posting all kinds of positions from all over the country, it's like having a stack of Sunday papers from all over America.

• *E-Span:* Another great database, E-Span was one of the first employment services opened online. Much like Help Wanted-USA, E-Span is searchable by keywords and contains jobs from all over the country.

CompuServe

Though it doesn't have nearly the career resources that America Online sports, CompuServe, a more business-oriented service, does have a few job assistance offerings.

Career Management Forum: Aside from hosting live chat sessions with career specialists, CompuServe's Career Management Forum provides a wide range of offerings, including reviews of job-assistance books, resume help and samples to go by, advice centers, a library of sample cover letters, and two bulletin boards (the Regional Talent library and the Relocatable Talent library) in which you can post your resume.

Using the World Wide Web

Welcome to Career Assistance Nirvana. Career advice on the Web is multiplying at an incredible rate, far beyond that of the major online services. An afternoon spent browsing some major for-profit and nonprofit career assistance Web sites, along with a printer full of paper, can equal hundreds of dollars' worth of professional career guidance and books on resumes and networking.

You'd have to have been under a rock during the past three years not to have heard about the World Wide Web, the multimedia portion of the Internet. The Internet itself has been around for about twenty-five years, having grown out of a group of connected networks set up by the U.S. Department of Defense and a handful of universities, but the Web made its debut in 1991.

Created by Tim Berners-Lee, a computer programmer at CERN (a European physics laboratory in Switzerland), even the Web remained a relatively quiet phenomenon until the creation in 1994 of Mosaic, a "browser," or piece of software that allows users to access windows of text, graphics, and sound in one document. Mosaic was created by Marc Andreessen, a graduate student at the University of Illinois-Champagne Urbana. (Now here's a great success story for those looking for inspiration: Andreessen was already worth hundreds of millions of dollars as a 23-year-old cofounder of Netscape.) Since then, it's been no turning back for the Web and the Internet. Jupiter estimates that over 13 million people had access to the Web in the United States alone in 1996, making it a true online community.

One of the beauties of the Web is that it gives everyone with a Web browser and access to an Internet service the ability to search a massive collection of resources, greater by far than those available on the online services. You can just about find everything under the sun on the Web today, but more importantly for people seeking to boost their job prospects, everything from resume services to interview advice to networking exists on the global network. With hundreds of pages of new data and content being added every hour, a person who can't find information on the Web just can't find information.

Entire books could be written on the wide sea of career sites, discussion groups, job listings, resume builders, talent banks, and posting boards, so we will touch on a few "megasites" here. And don't forget: A little time spent with a search engine on the Internet can also yield you some good starting points. Infoseek and Yahoo! both have separate listings of suggested career resources on the Web that can act as good starting points for your electronic job search.

JOBTRAK (www.jobtrak.com)

Launched in 1992, JOBTRAK caters to students who either are about to leave school or have just graduated and are beating the pavement for jobs. Aimed at universities, JOBTRAK adds more than 2,000 new job openings each day. It also claims that more than 200,000 employers use or have used the service to find graduates.

Among JOBTRAK's offerings are a place to post your resume for employers to read and the ability to update that resume when needed. A section called Job Search Tips gives practical advice on building your career; hundreds of jobs are made available for you to apply for, top recruiters are outlined, and a comprehensive description of major graduate school programs are available for those who want to extend their academic careers.

CareerMosaic (www.careermosaic.com)

Begun in 1995 by Bernard Hodes Advertising, a major human resources ad agency, CareerMosaic is representative of a class of job search and advice megasites on the Web. With recent expansion into Asia through CareerMosaic Japan, as well as into Canada and the United Kingdom, CareerMosaic presents users interested in pursuing international career possibilities a way to get in touch with overseas employers. CareerMosaic also features the Health Care Connection, a job service specifically geared toward this growing field.

Among the features on this service are CareerMosaic J.O.B.S., a frequently updated searchable database containing thousands of jobs; Employer Profiles, where you can get the low-down on businesses worldwide; the Career Resource Center, which provides job hunting information and resume tips; the College Connection for those still in school; and Online Job Fairs, where you can send your resume to a prospective employer while finding out more about the company.

The Monster Board (www.monster.com)

Another of the early job services on the Web, The Monster Board also sports a wide range of offerings. In its Career Center, The Monster Board offers Career Fairs, an online job fair where you can find out who will be recruiting in your area soon; Career Resources and Ask AL, two places for job advice; and a listing of other job help sites on the Web.

Other resources on The Monster Board include Career Surfari, where you can cruise over 55,000 jobs in the Monster Board database; Be The Boss; MedSearch, a health-care jobs database; and ROAR, a Generation X-oriented site where you can post your own literary output, chat with other young people, and search for entry-level positions.

CareerPath.com (www.careerpath.com)

CareerPath.com acts as a central database for job classifieds from newspapers in more than 20 different cities, including:

Atlanta Journal-Constitution
The Boston Globe
Chicago Tribune
The Columbus Dispatch
The Denver Post
Denver Rocky Mountain News
The Hartford Courant
Houston Chronicle
Los Angeles Times
The Miami Herald
Milwaukee Journal Sentinel
Minneapolis-St. Paul Pioneer Press
Minneapolis-St. Paul Star Tribune
The New York Times
The Orlando Sentinel
Philadelphia Inquirer
The Sacramento Bee
San Jose Mercury News
The Seattle Times/P-I
South Florida Sun-Sentinel
The Washington Post

CareerPath.com's listings boast more than 110,000 jobs at the time of this writing, and are growing at 10,000 ads per week. You must be a registered user to search CareerPath.com, but registration is simple and use of the site is free.

Virtual Job Fair (www.vjf.com)

Concentrating on high-tech jobs, Virtual Job Fair's database holds more than 15,000 job positions, searchable by job title, location, or company. More than 500 employers currently participate in Virtual Job Fair's service. Also available at this site is the Resume Center, allowing you to post your resume and have it converted to HTML, the language used to create Web pages, so that employers can see it in a public listing; or you may post it privately, revealing only your city, state, education, and skills.

Like any good site, the Virtual Job Fair also makes available career resources, such as lists of academic and special interest sites, federal and state government job resources, newsgroups, an employer database, a list of top Web sites, and other miscellaneous reference material.

A Final Word

Searching online for jobs and job information can be a fruitful endeavor. If you aren't yet comfortable with the Internet and don't quite know your way around, find a friend who can help guide you. With a little time and patience, you can be guaranteed to find a lot of information, and many good job leads.

Also, consider putting together an online resume. Most Internet accounts these days come with free Web space to put up your own Web pages. If you don't know HTML, the language of the Web, you can probably find a friend, fellow student, or neighbor who has a general understanding of it and knowledge of how to post documents online. Take a class and learn a little HTML. You may do wonders for your career, and it will look good on that online resume. Keep adding skills and spreading your job searching horizons and you will definitely be rewarded. Good luck!

CHAPTER 16

Your Prospective Employer: Knowing Your Prey

The job interview: perhaps the most feared part of everyone's employment life. But face it, we all have to go through job interviews to get where we want to be, from that first summer job baby-sitting or dishing out vanilla ice cream cones at the park to ascending to the post of Chairman of the Joint Chiefs of Staff. When you stop to think about it, what are presidential campaigns? They are the longest, most expensive job interviews in America, with the candidates groveling before 260,000,000 potential employers over a period of a year or more. Face it, no one gets away from job interviews, so we might as well take the optimist's view and get good at them.

Put simply, the reason we all dread interviews is because the interview process is the most critical step to getting a job, and career builders who handle the interview process well generally find themselves moving toward their career goals at a faster pace than those who don't. It's an ugly fact of life, but a fact nonetheless. It's a make-or-break process, and one that, like marriage, shouldn't be entered into lightly.

Notice the use of the words "interview process" above. That's right. Interviewing for a job is more than just showing up at an appointed time with your tie on straight and shoes shined. It has a beginning, a middle, and an end—hopefully, but not always, a successful one. The interview process starts long before the interview itself; first you must research the company. The process is a sometimes long, sometimes short courtship between you and the person or company that is going to trust you to successfully fulfill a mission, and in return support you financially for the length of your employment.

More critically—and this is something you will read more about later—for your future employer, the interview process represents a microcosm of how you will perform in the future, like a first date.

- Do you pay attention to detail?
- Are you punctual?
- Are you a perfectionist?
- Are you able to see a process through to its eventual conclusion?
- Are you a good negotiator?
- Can you do what you say you are capable of doing?
- Are you willing to take chances?

All of these questions can potentially be answered for your employer by the way you conduct yourself through the interview process, and often it is a process you must carry along on your own back, since employers today are looking for self-starters, people who will initiate a mission, keep it going, and end it successfully.

Know Your Prey

The first critical factor in the interview process, whether employers find you or you find them, is getting to know who they are, inside and out. No, you don't have to sit outside your future boss's house in an unmarked car with a video camera, but you do need to know who the person is, what the company's mission is, and so on. You want to know as much about your future employers as they will know about you, and it's almost certain your interviewers will be impressed by your initiative and ability to look them up and find out what makes them tick.

Here are some good questions to ask about a company in your preinterview research:

- Is it public (is its stock traded on an exchange) or privately held?
- How successful has it been? How stable is it financially?

- Has it had any recent problems (recent downsizing, big law suits, financing difficulties, officers resigning)?
- Has it announced any big initiatives lately (new products, new lines of business)?
- How does it treat its employees?
- How quickly does it promote employees?
- Does it like to hire from within, or does it have a history of looking elsewhere for talent?
- Who are its competitors?
- How does it stack up to its competitors?
- Where does the company appear to be headed?

Remember to give your future employer a good look, consider the information you unearth fairly, and consider it in light of your plans for the future. If a company has had recent problems, don't drop it from your list right away. Ask yourself, "Is it on the road to a turnaround?" If so, you may be able to get in on the ground floor of a new phase in your employer's future. If the company has recently downsized, there may be some morale problems, so be prepared for those as well.

If an employer doesn't look like a great long-term prospect, consider the opportunity in light of what you can get in terms of skills. Sometimes short stints of a year or two can help you build skills you need elsewhere, and short tenures at previous employers aren't looked at as negatively as they once were. Just remember, you need to be able to justify any short hops in future interviews. Be smart in your planning!

Hitting the Books

Where should you start your investigating? After all, your prospective employers have the advantage of having you fill out an application. Where can you find the same sort of information about a company? Again, turn to the resources around you: The public or school library, the newspaper, and the Internet and online services can be a boon to the person with a little time who is willing to put forward a little effort.

The Library

Far from being rendered useless by the Internet, your local library, whether it's on campus or in the public square, is chock-full of resources to help you find out more about potential employers. See Chapter 21 for some excellent resources in addition to those listed here.

Magazines and newspapers. Over the past few years, we've been so inundated by the spread of interactive communications and the proliferation of news on TV, it would be easy to think that newspapers and magazines had disappeared altogether. Not true. Our paper friends stacked on the bookshelf and the rolls of microfilm gathering dust in the corner are still the way most people performing research get their information, and considering the high cost of converting back catalogs of printed matter, and the investment schools and public libraries have made in gathering and archiving print periodicals, they are likely to remain the best way in the short term for the young person who doesn't have a free Lexis/Nexis account to get information about a potential employer's past history.

The United States has easily the best-researched and -documented business sector in the world. Literally hundreds of national magazines and journals cover public and private companies, and digging into past issues can provide a gold mine of information about potential employers. Some of the best national sources found in most libraries are:

The Wall Street Journal
The New York Times
The Financial Times
Barron's
USA Today
Investor's Business Daily
The Washington Post
The Los Angeles Times
The Chicago Tribune
The Christian Science Monitor

In addition, hundreds of daily papers from cities around the country carry good business news, and some often give a better picture of what a company is doing in your area or its home region.

Some good weekly and monthly magazines in which you will find articles about and comparisons of public and private companies are:

The Economist
Forbes
Fortune
U.S. News & World Report
Newsweek
Time
Business Week

And, of course, thousands of specialty magazines covering hundreds of areas of business, from national magazines such as *Inc.*, which looks at entrepreneurs, and *Restaurant News*, to regional publications such as *Atlanta Business Chronicle* or *Crain's Chicago Business*.

How Do I Find What I'm Looking For?

With all of the aforementioned piles of paper and microfilm facing you, how do you get to the bottom? There are two basic ways to accomplish the task: printed indices and databases. In older, less equipped libraries, printed indices have to do the trick. Most libraries, particularly at universities and colleges, will have a variety of databases you can use.

Printed indices. It seems a bit out of date these days to find anything in a dusty, old book, but prior to the early to mid-1980s, believe it or not, that's how it was done for many magazines. Luckily, newspapers' indices have been available on microfilm a bit longer. Many major national magazines printed bound indices by year, and in many larger or university libraries, they are placed at the end of the rows of a particular magazine's bound back issues. Sometimes they can be found in the reference sections as well. Many good magazines have the subjects of articles arranged alphabetically. Just take a dive in and find the name of the company you are researching and ask the librarian to help you find the relevant magazine and issue.

Microfilm. As mentioned above, newspapers, particularly national ones, have been available on microfilm for quite a while. In this instance, as may also be the case with magazines, you will probably have to start with some sort of database. Indices, as well as the actual copy of the publication, will be on microfilm. Later models of microfilm machines allow you to print the pages you need directly from the machine.

Databases. These days, a wide variety of databases are available at larger libraries. There are a number of basic periodical databases on the market, many of them based on CD-ROM, that allow you to select a time frame you wish to search (example: magazines from January 1, 1994, to December 31, 1994), and often give you a choice of the types of periodicals to search. By entering selected "key" words, you can find all articles written about or containing reference to the company in question.

EDGAR. If you are really interested in the financial details on a company, you can use EDGAR, a database made available to the public by the Securities and Exchange Commission, the federal agency that regulates all publicly traded companies. EDGAR contains public companies' quarterly and annual financial reports, along with other data, including the salaries of corporate officers (always valuable data to have in the back of your head in an interview). If you don't understand financial reports (and not many people do!), get a friend or faculty member to help you sort them out. Sometimes this information can tell you a lot about the state of a company, including its future prospects.

■ Sources of Information Within the Company Itself

Just about every company with a payroll over twenty-five people has either a public relations department or a person whose job it is to field questions about the company.

The Public Relations Department

After you've done a little investigative research at the local library, it doesn't hurt to give your target company's public relations department a call and ask for an information packet. This could give you valuable information about how the company views itself and what it wants the rest of the world to know and think about it. Recent initiatives and future plans are often outlined in press releases, and your future projects just may be described as well.

The Investor Relations Office

Nearly all publicly traded companies have an investor relations department or officer. The information available from this department is generally a combination of what the SEC's EDGAR database can tell you and what you will hear from a public relations department. Again, you can get recent financial information about the company, including a copy of the most recent annual report, and give it a look to find out more.

The Internet and Online Services

If you do have access to the Internet or a service like America Online or CompuServe, there are a lot of ways you can look up companies. If you have World Wide Web access, many companies both large and small, public and private, now have pages in cyberspace, and a little searching here first may save you some time at the library.

Search Engines

You may have learned on television or in a magazine about so-called search engines on the Web, and you may have even used one or more of them already. As the Web grows, these engines send out "robot" programs to scour the Web in search of new pages of information. Some, like Lycos, have millions or tens of millions of pages on servers across the planet, cataloged and ready for retrieval at your request. All you have to do is launch a Web browser, type in the relevant address (some samples are given below), follow the search instructions on the search engine's home page, and let the power of armies of high-speed servers and processors do the walking for you.

Some good search engines are located at the following addresses on the World Wide Web:

Infoseek Guide	www.infoseek.com	Great for general searches
Yahoo!	www.yahoo.com	Organized by categories
Lycos	www.lycos.com	Gives quick reviews of pages
Excite	www. excite.com	Similar to Lycos; reviews
AltaVista	altavista.dec.com	High-speed power searches

The results of a search with a search engine can be astounding and very informative. Often you will get a mix of firsthand information from the company itself mixed in with articles referencing the company from the many publications that are now online. For example, a search for "Exxon" might yield one or more of the pages on the Exxon corporate Web site, as well as a number of articles from places like *The New York Times* or bits from a college student's Web page on oil companies or chunks from a research paper, or even rants against Exxon from an environmental group. You might get a jumble of good and bad information, but thirty minutes spent with an Internet search engine can pay off immensely.

Stand-Alone Web Resources

A number of resources other than search engines are springing up on the Web as well. As mentioned above, a number of publications are now up and running on the Web, with back archives available for research. In addition, some traditional print publications, such as *Hoover's Company Profiles*, are now available on the Web.

Hoover's in particular maintains an excellent resource on the Web at www. hoovers.com. On this site you can find in-depth descriptions of thousands of companies, what each one's business is, who its competitors are, and financial information; there are also profiles of new companies, a look at their stock offerings, and links to more than 2,700 corporate Web sites around the globe.

Online Services

Online services such as America Online are now beginning to provide links to similar information. *Hoover's Company Profiles* also maintains a presence on America Online, offering similar information to that available on its Web site. These offerings include stock information, financial statements, past earnings and earning estimates, and access to the SEC's EDGAR service. This area can be reached on America Online by entering the key words "company research."

What to Do With What You've Found

Once you've turned up all of the information you feel you need, it's time to put it all together, carefully read through it, and draw up a list of questions to take to your interview. Any good interviewer won't forget to ask you at the end of an interview whether you have any questions, and you should have a few prepared. Remember, you are checking the company out too, and asking a few insightful questions about the direction of the company, whom it perceives its competitors to be, and so on will never lose you points with a good interviewer.

Researching Salaries

Just as important as gathering information on prospective employers is knowing how much you are worth to them. Whether it is in the first interview or weeks later, the issue of salary will come up at some point, and it is critical that you know at least in a rough sense what your chosen field and position is paying in your city or region of the country.

As with company data, there are a number of resources available to help you find out what the trends in pay and benefits are by profession and geographical area. There are many reference books and articles available from the library and bookstores that can help you decide where you fall in terms of salary, such as Arsen Darnay's *American Salaries and Wages Annual Survey*. Also, the *Occupational Outlook Handbook* is often of great use and can be found in many libraries' reference sections. The Bureau of Labor Statistics' *Occupational Compensation Survey* is available in many libraries and online as well, and tells you how much people holding similar positions earn in different regions of the country.

As is the case in any information search, don't be shy about asking professionals to help you. Reference librarians at most large public and university libraries are more than willing to point you in the right direction, and most large bookstores maintain an information desk for much the same purpose. Take advantage of their knowledge.

And one very important hint: Stay organized. It's very easy to forget the status of the dozens of simultaneous inquiries you're bound to make. You should use a computer database program (or plain old index cards if a computer isn't available) and keep track of every correspondence or discussion you have with every prospective employer. Keep track of the name, title, address, and phone number of each contact person; each date that you make contact with that person and

his or her colleagues in the future; and detailed instructions for your next step in the job search process (call again next week, send another copy of the resume, and so on). The worst thing that can happen is that you will receive a call from someone and not remember from which company that person is returning your call. Not having the information you need at your fingertips can cost you a job very quickly.

How Much Will You Need?

As you are checking to see how much you are worth, also take into consideration how much you need to earn to make a reasonable living. Unless you are very lucky, you won't be buying a Porsche or even a BMW on that first salary. Take into consideration your living arrangements, such as rent, commuting, clothing, and food requirements (clothing—plus dry cleaning—is especially important to consider if you are taking a job where you may need a number of good suits or dresses, such as in a professional firm or a bank).

Also consider that, under the current tax structure, you will be taking home something on the order of 65 to 75 percent of your total gross salary, and that doesn't include possible deductions for items like health care and a 401(k) retirement plan, both of which employees must often contribute to in whole or in part. Thus, a salary of $36,000 gross annually may only get you a monthly total of $2,000 in your pocket before bills, rent, and so on. This may seem like a lot, but $2,000 a month can disappear in a hurry, particularly in urban areas. So, remember, find out what you are worth, decide on what you need, and settle on a range of salaries you think is fair and reasonable.

More will be said later on how to deal with salary negotiations, but it is important to have a range of figures in mind before you really even begin the search for a job, much less before you sit down at the table to talk turkey with an interviewer. As with buying a car, you need to enter the "showroom" armed with some information of your own.

CHAPTER 17

Getting Ready for the Interview

Once you've gathered the skinny on your prospective employer, it's time to face the music, as it were. Literally hundreds of books, and now a good number of online resources, tell you how to master the interview itself, and many agree on some fundamentals: be confident, be prepared, look the interviewer in the eye, dress for success, and so on. None of those will be disputed here, but a few points of great importance are emphasized below, with some time-tested techniques and pointers laid out for your consumption.

And remember, just as not every person is a good interviewee, not every interviewer is up to the task either, and not all of them play fair. It is important to know this from the outset, however, and not let yourself get sidetracked with mind games or personality issues. In more than 90 percent of all interviews, if you are prepared and are a reasonable match for the job, you should be able to place yourself in contention for a position if you want it.

And most fundamental of all, no interview is a wasted effort! Every interview experience, successful or not, is one you can learn from when facing future situations. Like a good athlete, you should prepare, play the game to the best of your ability, and "watch the film" afterwards, which is to say you should think back through the entire interview and analyze your performance with an eye toward doing better next time around.

Prepare for Tough Questions

Unless your interviewer is asleep or has already decided you are the right candidate for the job, you will be asked a series of questions, some easy, some hard, that are generally designed not only to give an interviewer a good idea of how well you have memorized your resume, but how well you think on your feet, how you react to surprises, how clearly you think, how you see yourself, how you handle tough scenarios, and generally how articulate you are. In the minds of many interviewers, your performance on the spot in an interview gives them a good idea of how you will perform in the future.

With these points in mind, it's best to sit down well in advance of an interview and think through possible questions that might be asked by the interviewer. Many of them are predictable, and if you haven't gone through a typical job interview before, friends and family members can probably fill you in on the basic questions. Some of the all-time favorites you are almost certain to encounter are:

- **"Tell me about yourself."** There is no need to launch into an in-depth family history at the asking of this question. Generally, interviewers use this question as something of an ice breaker to get the interview going. It helps you both get comfortable, and it often gives you a point of mutual interest from which to start. This is a question often asked to see how well you summarize information and describe yourself. Give the important details but be concise. Talk about where you went to school, what work experience you have had, your leisure activities and hobbies, and so on. Recap your resume without doing the big sell job.

- **"Why did you choose to major in primate studies in college?"** Another icebreaker question designed to find out how you have set out your path in life. More and more, students are leaving school with degrees in areas they will not pursue in professional life, including such liberal arts favorites as psychology, history, English, sociology and the emerging regional and cultural studies degrees.

If you are not directly applying the education on which you might have spent thousands or tens of thousands of dollars, be prepared to explain why and how your skills and background relate to the business of the person sitting across the desk from you. Think about how your education relates to what you are asking someone to spend thousands of dollars to let you do.

- **"Why do you want to come to work for BurgerWorld International?"** Think this one through carefully. This question is one of the main reasons for doing a little research into the company beforehand. You may want to mention how you want to work for a world-class family-style food franchising organization to learn mass food delivery from the acknowledged leader in the field, but nine out of ten of the other candidates vying for the job will also give this kind of answer.

Do a little homework, and let your interviewer know you know a bit about the company, such as how you want to work for the aforementioned leader in food delivery that has improved efficiency by 50 percent over the past three years, has raised profits in a recession-hit industry, and is preparing to make the kind of investments in high-tech information systems that you have experience maintaining and/or would like to gain experience installing.

- **"Why do you want to leave your job at the International House of Coffee to join BurgerWorld? After all, you've been there for only eighteen months."** Another golden oldie of the interview process, but one that must be negotiated carefully. Never, under any conditions, badmouth your previous employer in an interview, no matter how bad things may have been. It can't be said enough, going on a job interview is like going on a first date: Stay positive and don't talk about past failures. If you speak negatively about your previous employer, how does your interviewer know that you won't do the same to your future employer down the road?

In short, it's always best to take the high ground, because it is the most defensible position. Although you can't explain a job change without giving the reason why, you can avoid dishing dirt on a previous boss.

Example:

> **Interviewer:** " I hear things aren't going well over at IHOC. Are you getting out before things get bad?"

You: "Not really. I have been considering this sort of move for a while, and I want to work for a company that gives me the opportunity to move ahead and apply my skills in kitchen ergonomics, something I didn't feel I would be able to do in the near-term at IHOC."

• **"What would you say are your best and worst qualities?"** Interviewers should be banned from asking this one, but it is still used frequently, probably because it has such pat answers that you are hardpressed to get it right. It is sort of a self-incrimination exercise. The usual answers go something like "My best quality is that I am punctual, and my worst quality is probably that I am a perfectionist."

Yuck! Think this one through for days. It is probably one of the best opportunities you have for either impressing the interviewer or nailing the lid down tight on your own coffin. Be honest, be candid, but above all, be careful. If hired, you will probably be reminded of your answers six months down the road when you have neither been punctual nor detailed in your work.

As for positive qualities, interviewers like to hear that you tend to lead rather than to follow, that you are a good problem solver, that you manage yourself and/or others well, that you are creative (in the right circumstances), that you are detail-oriented, or that you are persistent. These qualities matter more today as companies slice away layers of management and rely on employees more and more to manage themselves and the teams in which they now often work.

They don't care as much that you are easygoing, or even that you are punctual, because many companies are also moving to flexible schedules. There is a line of people outside the interviewer's door who can get up in the morning and catch a bus. The qualities that companies generally want are reliability and leadership. They want someone they can count on to deliver the goods with a minimum of maintenance.

• **"Why should we hire you?"** Yet another time-tested question. Interviewers should already know the answer to this one themselves, but they just want to make you explain for the hundredth time why you are sure you are the right person for the job. Before you enter an interview, you should have thought this question through. Think about why you want the job, what you can bring to it, what it will teach you, and what makes you different from anyone else who has interviewed for the position. If you have unique skills, now is the time to reiterate that you have them. Don't be a broken record, but drive the point home thoughtfully, yet strongly.

- **"Most of our work requires us to use PCs running an old version of Microsoft Windows. Will that be a problem for you?"** Yes, it's the dreaded technology question. The key thing to remember here is that if you are asked about your proficiency on certain types of computers or programs, be honest but express your willingness to learn.

If you have used a Macintosh all your life and you are faced with an all-PC company (which is a good possibility), react positively. "No, I haven't worked on a PC before, but I am interested in mastering the Windows system," would be an appropriate response. Whatever you do, if you want the job, don't close the door on something you aren't familiar with. If you say no, you may very well take yourself out of the running. Turn your weaknesses into potential for growth and opportunities to learn.

- **"How much do you want to earn?" ("What kind of salary are you looking for?")** Look out, because these are dangerous waters. The big fear for interviewees is that they don't want to trip themselves before they even get in the door. Nonetheless, there aren't many easy ways out of this one.

As said at the end of Chapter 16, it is of the utmost importance that you enter in the interview process well armed with some salary information and well aware of how much you need to earn. The best strategy to follow is to be honest, and try not to gauge much by the interviewer's expression; it can't be said enough that many interviewers themselves aren't good at handling interview situations, and are doing a part of their job they often aren't trained for. They very often have to go back to their boss and discuss the situation, so your life may well not be in the hands of the person in front of you.

When faced with this question, it is often effective to simply say something to the effect of, "Well, considering the type of work I will be doing, the size of this company, and the market value for this position in this area, I would say I am interested in a position that pays in the range of $X to $Y." If you know the range the employer is looking for, job counselors often advise you to take the top of the employer's range and add $5,000 to it. This says that you are serious about the position, but it also gives you some room to play with. Let the interviewer know you are aware of the market for the job, and that you have done your homework in deciding how much *you* think you are worth to the company. A good interviewer will respect you for playing it straight and not beating around the bush. Although you may feel as if you have laid your cards out on the table too early, you will be better off in the long run for having aired the issue.

Other Questions

There are probably hundreds of other questions you will get hit with in your interview besides those listed above. The key to handling questions about yourself is to remain positive, don't be afraid to hesitate for a moment to compose your answer, and be genuine and practical. If you are frank and open with your interviewer, and are willing to admit you have made mistakes but are ready to provide ways you would avoid mistakes again or solve problems, you should be in good shape when you leave the interview. Above all, *don't lie*! Fibbing to an interviewer will almost always come back to bite you, and can be found out easily during a reference check. Be honest on your resume, and tell it straight to an interviewer. Lying can not only cost you a chance at the job, but news travels among professionals, and you may find your letters to other employers in the area unanswered.

Behavioral Interviewing

A recent trend in job interviewing is a technique known as behavioral interviewing. Human resources specialist Joseph Stimac describes behavioral interviewing in his "Winning Career Strategies" training program as questioning that aims to predict your future behavior on the job on the basis of your previous job experiences. Rather than ask you a hypothetical question such as "How would you react to an angry customer?" Stimac says an interviewer who wants to determine how you would react on the job would ask you to tell of an experience in the past where you were confronted by an angry customer, and also to tell how you dealt with that customer.

Stimac says that traditional hypothetical questioning allows for hypothetical models to be built about what you might or might not do on the job in the future, but it is not often an indicator of how you would really react in different situations. As pointed out above, it is easy to give a sunny answer to a tough question, but an interviewer gets little out of your answers, other than determining how smart you think the interviewer is, or how unprepared you are for the interview.

Behavioral interviewing provides an opportunity for the interviewer to find out not only how you reacted to past events, but how you handle tough questioning, particularly related questions about an issue. An example of this would be a chain of questions that might begin with something like "Have you ever missed a deadline?" then move to a related question, such as "How did you deal with that situation?" or "What lessons did you learn from missing that deadline?"

Behavioral interviewing can be tough, because it does require you to focus your responses and consider them in light of the overall interview. If your interviewer does launch into this kind of questioning, don't panic. Take the time to prepare here as well. Think through negative or difficult situations, as well as how you dealt with them. Ask yourself those tough, searching questions and think though the most constructive, honest way to answer them.

Such preparation will undoubtedly pay off in the interview. And be prepared to relate positive experiences as well. Not all interviewers are out to trip you up or expose past difficulties. What they want to know is that you think clearly, understand situations in their entirety, and know how to learn from them and make changes based on past experience.

Practicing Before Your Interview

Just as with taking an important exam in school, you don't want to go into an interview half-prepared. Set out a list of hard questions for yourself and think through how you would answer them, and where those answers could potentially lead the interviewer. Sit down in front of a mirror or with a relative or friend and practice answering them.

Go over them time and time again, and practice different ways of wording responses until you find answers you are comfortable with. You need to come across sincerely, and interviewers will know if you are bluffing. Often a second question on a subject on which you have put yourself out on a limb will catch you in an intellectual cul-de-sac.

Eye contact is of utmost importance in an interview, and this can't be emphasized enough. Maintaining eye contact is important because it lets the interviewer know both that you are interested and paying close attention to his or her questions, and that you are not timid or afraid. Test after test has shown that when people avert their eyes or look down during a question and answer session, the perception is that the interviewee is uncomfortable with the questioning or is not telling the truth.

You will know ahead of time if you have a tendency to look away when answering or dart your eyes around the room. This is why it is so important that you practice in front of a mirror or with parents or friends, to check your behavior and get comfortable looking your interviewer straight in the eye.

CHAPTER 18

How Not to Blow the Big Moment

It is very important to realize early on in life that success boils down to the individual. It doesn't matter if you have a 4.0 grade point average in computers from an Ivy League school; if you don't have a positive attitude, nothing will help you secure a career and, more importantly, you won't feel personally fulfilled in your life's ambition. The bottom line will always come down to what type of person you are. Attitude makes the winners as well as the losers.

Developing the right attitude is an elemental task, but it should not be confused with an easy one. For a Buddhist, reaching his or her utopia, or Zen state, is a simple task, but it is not easy. The mind is very complex; some thoughts can be very destructive without the individual even knowing it.

One of the most common mistakes a person makes when entering a highly stressful situation is not visualizing it positively, through the use of affirmations. Most people when they walk into a job interview, for example, will say to themselves, "Please don't let me mess up." Unfortunately that little phrase is a counteraffirmation and therefore a counterproductive way of thinking.

The use of the negative phrase "mess up" will send you down the wrong attitude path. Some of you are probably surprised that we didn't cite the word "don't" as the operative negative word in the sentence. Words like "don't" are negative, but the brain does not react to them. Let us prove this point. Right now we don't want you to think of blue whales cresting the ocean's surface and splashing back down into the water.

Did you visualize a whale that was blue, becoming airborne and falling back into the sea? Of course you did. See our point? Words like "can't," "won't," "shouldn't," and "never" fail to counter the brain's focus on the crux of the sentence.

So when you say to yourself, "Please don't let me mess up," what you are really saying is, "Please let me mess up."

Dr. Harville Hendrix, an author of many books on psychology, explains that the brain sends messages to the body based upon what the thought is. If you think of winning the lottery, the body will feel a tide of euphoria, equal to the strength of that thought. If you really, truly believed (with no physical evidence) that you won the American Family Publishers sweepstakes, chances are you'd be jumping up and down right now and looking around for Ed McMahon or Dick Clark and wanting to kiss them on the cheek. Thoughts like these, and believing in them, are what make the brain so powerful.

But back to our example with the interviewee. Because the brain doesn't pick up the word "don't," this person sent a thought to the brain that said, "Please let me mess up," and the brain sent the same message to the body. So when that person walked into the interview, he or she was already feeling as though he or she had stumbled and the interview was lost before it was even begun.

A better way to approach interviews (or life for that matter) is getting comfortable with using positive thoughts. Notions like "I'm the best candidate for the job" or "With my winning smile, they're bound to love me" will greatly improve your chances of success and also will put a little spring into your step. Because, as was already discussed, the body will feel what the brain tells it to: Why not make it something positive?

Thinking positively is something that comes naturally to a child; becoming an adult usually makes it more difficult to think this way. Bringing back positive thoughts takes effort. Here are some positive thoughts that can help you move back to the positive side:

- I'm ready to begin my career.
- I'm capable of performing any task brought to me on the job.
- I'm well liked among my peers.
- I welcome the changes that are coming in the workplace and will thrive in this new environment.
- I'm confident in my decisions and state them soundly.
- I love learning about new technologies that are sweeping the job market.
- I recognize that the skills I possess, if implemented within this company, would do them a great service.
- This company needs me in a bad way.
- I'm resourceful and can find opportunities where other fail to see them.
- I'm capable of anything and everything; watch out!

Bob Fosse, a famous and very talented performer, right before going on stage, used to look at himself in the mirror, smile his biggest smile, open his eyes their widest, and say the word, "*Showtime!!*" This was the affirmation that prompted his visualization of being talented that made his body feel like a million bucks, and when he took the stage, he owned it.

Some people will feel that you're being cocky or conceited when working these affirmations; let them think that. The best and the brightest know how important a strong, healthy self-image is to becoming a success in one's chosen field. Anyone who pokes fun usually is someone not worth listening to.

The world is changing, and as Darwin first said, usually the strongest survive these changes. In our case that means being in possession of not only an educated mind, but also one that thinks and feels like a winner.

Here are some tips for the *big meeting* itself.

Dress to Show You Mean It

As you approach interview day—armed of course with lots of information in your head and briefcase, as well as prepared for tough questions—you need to think about the other critical part of your presentation: your appearance. Interview dress used to be a nonissue;

everyone wore a conservative suit or dress for every occasion. But the radical changes that American business culture has undergone in the past twenty years have made deciding how to dress for an interview, as well as most other components of interview protocol, nearly anyone's call.

Dressing for an interview today comes down to the profession you are pursuing, the city or region you live in or are interviewing in, and a wide range of other factors that may seem totally arbitrary. Graphic designers in New York dress very differently for an interview than they do in Omaha, and those interviewing for a job with a Manhattan-based magazine often look very different from those looking for a job with a bank in Atlanta or an advertising agency in Cheyenne. So much of how you carry yourself in an interview, not only your dress but your demeanor, is dictated by the situation and the environment surrounding the interview.

It can't be said enough: It's important to talk to your friends, if you have any in the profession in question, or others who have been through the same or similar situations. They can often give you the straight dope on what a particular employer likes or dislikes, cutting down on your guesswork.

Another thing that can't be stressed enough is that, when in doubt about how you should approach a job interview, you should choose more conservative dress and protocol. Unless you are interviewing in a field where creativity is the most valued skill, such as in some art fields, conservative dress will minimize any risk of inappropriate dress, and its result: starting the interview off from a negative position. Men should wear a neutral-colored suit, simple tie, and neat-looking shoes. Women should wear a suit or conservative dress, with little jewelry, makeup, or perfume. Pumps are usually preferable to stiletto heels; your goal is to look neat and practical, not sexy.

As with most issues surrounding employment and interviewing, there are many good magazines and books on the market describing how you can dress in a way that will help you in an interview. Remember, the interview is the first impression the interviewer will have of you in person. Save the relaxed or eccentric look for when you have had time to gauge the appropriate mode of dress at your new workplace. Show the interviewer some respect by the way you dress and carry yourself, and it will pay off.

In this area, keep in mind that your appearance is not dictated just by clothing. In college you may have dyed your hair blue and worn a nose ring. It's time to separate yourself from this past. Corporate America, despite some notable advances, is still pretty stodgy. If you want this community to welcome you, you have to look the part—and the part is pretty plain.

■ Punctuality Is Not Optional

Interviewing for employment is a practice full of variables, as we have seen above. What time to arrive for an interview is one of them, though it is only variable to a point. Whatever you do, whether you have an excuse or not, *do not be late for an interview*! Being late tells interviewers a number of things, such as you don't plan very well, you don't value their time (which they most likely will), and you will likely not value getting to work on time or meeting deadlines in the future.

Just as you prepare for interview questions and try on your outfit the night before to make sure it has no holes, know where you are going for your interview and make the trip at least once to make sure you know how to get there, how long it takes, whether there are any potential obstacles to getting there on time, and so on. Championship cyclists, runners, skaters, and other athletes always get on the track ahead of a race, and then walk, run, cycle, or skate it to make sure they know the lay of the land. Getting a job you want should be as important to you as winning the gold medal in the 100-meter hurdles.

Another issue that is debated is when to arrive. While it might seem sensible to arrive very early to avoid any possibility of being late, some interviewers find prospects who arrive thirty minutes early and sit in the reception area reading *Forbes* an annoyance. A number of employers we have spoken to feel rushed if the interviewee arrives too early.

By the same token, many companies will have you fill out some sort of formal application for their records, which may take a few minutes in advance of the interview. Also, consider the weather conditions, whether you have to climb a large number of stairs, how tough parking might be if you are driving, and so on; and try to give yourself time to cool down from hot and humid weather outside, calm down from a hectic commute, negotiate a parking deck, or catch your breath from running the stairs.

No one wants to interview a red-faced, sweaty, or gasping prospect. Take the time to aim your arrival at ten minutes or so before the appointed interview time so that you can relax and prepare. Again, good planning will pay off in the end.

At the Table

If you are smart, you have now spent a few days reading up on the company, mentally rehearsing the interview, staying relaxed, picking out a good outfit, and checking the route to the interview. You are now past the receptionist, shaking hands with your potential employer, and sitting down at the table. What can you do now to keep things on track?

A few pointers not mentioned above will help you navigate the dark waters of the interview itself.

- *Remain relaxed*. Once you have gotten in the door, it's no time for sweaty palms, a dry mouth, and a blank mind. Take a deep breath on the way in the door, smile, be personable, and things should be fine. One note: Avoid a big cup of coffee before the interview. Besides making you need to use the restroom, coffee can cause you to be overly chatty, bouncing your leg around under the table, and bending paper clips until they break. Moreover, caffeine makes some people hot and jittery and gives them dry mouth. Save the double espresso for after the big event.
- *Listen carefully*. Your mind may be racing, and interviews require you to do a lot of thinking while you or someone else is talking: examining the situation, thinking through answers and strategies, and so on. In short, the mind of an interviewee is a very noisy place during the big event. Keep on top of things, but most of all, *listen carefully*. Coming off as not paying attention can be bad for business in this situation.
- *Keep it to the point*. You will doubtless have a lot of questions thrown your way, some easy, some difficult. The keys to a good answer are being concise and brief. Answer the question that was asked by the most direct route, even though it may require an illustrative example to get you there. Don't ramble just to fill dead air, and listen to where you are going with your answers. Many people babble when they are nervous, and some of us are given to making silly statements to defuse a tense situation. Hit the highlights.
- *Be positive and enthusiastic, but don't be annoying*. Employers like to know a future hire is going to be a go-getter, enthusiastic and positive. Nobody likes a dead fish or a dullard on the team. Keep your energy level up, but keep it under control.
- *Be polite and professional*. Consider the interviewer a valued colleague, as he or she may one day be. You wouldn't call your minister Bob, or your boyfriend or spouse's parents Phil and Sandy on the first meeting, nor should you take a familiar tone with your interviewer right away (unless you are friends beforehand). As with what

you wear, how you speak tells the interviewer about your level of respect for him or her.

Start out with Mr. or Ms. on the first go-around, and let the interviewer set the tone. He or she will let you know if things should be more familiar. Be sure to thank everyone, and be sure to get a business card from each person you interview with, both at the first interview and at subsequent ones. Not only does this help you get in touch with people for follow-up questions, it provides you with the correct names, titles, and addresses for thank-you letters, which are discussed in more detail in Chapter 19.

CHAPTER 19

Asking Your Own Questions

A job interview is a two-way street, and you should be prepared with questions of your own. You interviewer will expect you to ask some questions, and will think more of you if you come with a number of good questions in hand. Not only do they give you a good idea about the particular job and company, they give you specific information by which you can compare the position to others you may be considering. Questions about advancement, benefits, overtime, and so on will also help you evaluate the salary that may be offered. Some of the important ones to ask are:

• *"Exactly what does this job entail?"* This is a crucial question to ask if the details haven't been explicitly laid out for your by you interviewer. You want to leave the first interview knowing exactly what the job is all about. You could even ask whether there's a written job description you could see.

• *"What are the advancement opportunities for this position*?" Inquiring about advancement serves at least two purposes: It lets you know what your next logical step(s) would be at Company X, and it tells your interviewer that you are an ambitious and motivated person, looking ahead while considering what is currently on the table. However, be careful: You don't want to seem so ambitious that you'll be restless and dissatisfied with the job you're applying for within a few months. Even if this is true, keep it to yourself! Be sure to convey enthusiasm about the job you're *now* applying for.

• *"Can you tell me more about the company?"* Though you may already know quite a lot from your research, this question gives the interviewer an opportunity to tell you more and lets you hear the story from his or her perspective.

• *"Can you tell me more about this department and the work it does?"* Asking this question provides a good opportunity for the interviewer to sketch out the structure of the department you are being interviewed to join, and how it fits into the overall structure of the company.

• *"Who do you consider your competitors to be?"* Again, though you may already have a good idea about how the company is positioned within the industry and seen from the outside world, it is important to hear the story from the company's perspective. The answer can sometimes be illuminating, and it gives you a chance to see how the company views itself.

• *"What are your goals for this position?"* This is a very important question to put to your interviewer. Though the interviewer may have already described the position and what it entails, this question should help you find out just what is expected from the person who holds this position, and it opens a window on what your employer expects from you should you be offered and accept the job.

• *"Can you describe the reporting or management structure of this division or department?"* This question allows you to see the position in question as it relates to other members of the department or division. Not only will you find out to whom you report and in what order, you can determine how your position interrelates with the other members of the department or division.

• *"What is communication like in this department?"* Again, this kind of question provides an opportunity for the interviewer to fully lay out the structure of the position and department. It will also give the interviewer a chance to describe in his or her own words how well the department functions and what you should expect in terms of communication from your superiors and co-workers.

• *"Are there opportunities for lateral movement or transfer?"* Like the question about advancement, this question shows that you are interested in diversity of work and also lets you find out how the company or department is structured. Many companies today are replacing fewer opportunities to move up with more opportunities to cross-train and move to areas that may be on the same rung of the corporate structure.

• *"How will I be evaluated?"* As with the above question concerning goals for a particular position, this question gives you a chance to find out what are considered to be the benchmarks for a job well done at the company in question.

• *"Is overtime frequent?"* Questions about workload and overtime are important, and a good interviewer will know what you are asking. If you are going to be able to adequately evaluate a salary and benefits package, you need to know what the hours will be. Some companies, particularly smaller ones, sometimes don't manage the time of their employees well, or are chronically understaffed. This question may help you evaluate this possibility as well.

• *"What percentage of my time will be spent on different parts of my job?"* Again, this question probes further into the job in question and helps you find out what it is all about. Will you spend 80 percent of your time doing menial labor and 20 percent on the things that interest you? Asking this can not only help you find out the division of labor, it gives you something to hold your future employer to when "mission-creep," or extra duties, find their way into your working life.

Sealing the Deal: Following the First Interview

Nothing can be quite as satisfying as, or disheartening than, the moments following the first interview for any job. If things went well, or if you did poorly, you will generally know from the reaction of the interviewer. Most interviewers who plan to call you back will let you know that you should expect to hear from them, and will often give you a time frame for their reply.

If they do not, it is not considered impolite to ask whether you should expect to get a call, and whether you can supply the interviewer with any additional information, such as references or work samples. Remember to be assertive without being pushy, always smile no matter what the situation, and thank the interviewer, his or her receptionist or assistant, and anyone else you might have encountered.

Saying Thank You

Once you have come out of the interview, it's time to breathe free for a minute, relax, and reflect on your experience—sort of a personal debriefing. But don't get too comfortable. The first thing you should do, after you ditch that tie or kick off those high heels, is sit down and write thank-you letters to your interviewers.

This may sound like an old-fashioned thing to do, and in a way it is. Although this custom isn't widely practiced anymore in job interviews, it is widely seen by employers as an important indication of your sincerity and attitude as an interviewee. It is very possible that other candidates for the position for which you have interviewed have followed protocol and sent thank-you letters. If you skip this step, your competitors for the position in question—though equally or maybe even slightly less qualified—will likely have a higher place in the interviewer's mind.

Obtaining your interviewers' business cards is important because it will allow you to get your letters to them quickly. Though you can send your letter by mail, often thank-you letters are faxed on the same day as the interview. E-mail, however, is not yet suggested. Though it gets your message to the interviewer immediately, many people still see e-mail as a less formal mode of communication.

What should the letter say? Postinterview thank-you letters are a simple affair and should be kept short and to the point. See the sample of a typical thank-you letter on page 109.

The thank-you letter really serves several purposes above and beyond just saying thanks. Primarily, it shows that you are sincerely interested in the position in question, and that you would like to remain in serious contention. It also serves as an opportunity to reinforce messages you imparted during the interview: that you have a real interest in this line of work, that you feel you are uniquely qualified to fill the position, that you are willing to do what is necessary to fulfill and exceed the employer's expectations for the position—though all of these things should be put tactfully rather than pounded into the reader's head.

As with any other written communication between you and a prospective employer, proofread your letter carefully. Your resume and cover letter got you in the door and you handled yourself well in the interview. Don't get sloppy now and send a letter with typos or poor grammar. The thank-you letter should be the final bow after a good performance.

Following Up With Calls

Depending upon the hiring timeline your interviewer set out at your interview (an important question to ask in the interview), if you haven't heard back from your interviewer in a reasonable amount of time, a few days to a week later you should call to check up on your status as a candidate. This is another instance where you must balance keeping your profile up with the employer and not annoying him or her.

In nearly all cases, a simple call to the main interviewer to check on your status should suffice. Calling to make sure the employer has all the information he or she needs to make the decision should be enough to let that person know you are still interested in the position. In some cases, the follow-up call can help dislodge the logjam on the interviewer's desk. Remember, employers are very busy and can get bogged down, too.

Sample letter

November 23, 1997

Mr. Bill Johnson
Vice President
Sales & Marketing
ABC Health Care Supplies
1234 Broad Street
Peoria, IL 56789

Dear Mr. Johnson:

I want to thank you for taking the time to meet with me today and to allow me to share with you my background and skills. Also, thank you for discussing with me the needs, goals, and marketing priorities of ABC Health Care. I appreciate having the chance to speak with you about ABC's current opportunities, and how I can help you take advantage of them. I also appreciate your sharing with me your experiences starting out in this field.

As I mentioned in our discussion, I have a great interest in the health care market, having focused my senior research project on the marketing of medical products, and feel well prepared to apply my knowledge of the industry and to add to it through firsthand experience expanding the sales of ABC.

If I can supply you with any further information or answer any questions for you, please do not hesitate to contact me. Again, thank you for the opportunity to visit with you and the world-class staff at ABC, and I look forward to hearing from you soon.

Sincerely,

Tom Baker

cc:file

CHAPTER 20

You're Evaluating Them, Too

If all goes well, after one, two, or even three interviews, you will receive the phone call, letter, or e-mail you have been waiting for offering you a position. This is a great feeling, but the process of getting the job doesn't stop here. There are still a few things to do, such as discussing salary and benefits, and accepting the position (which means more than just shouting *"Okay!"* on the telephone).

But if you have not had much success in getting a job, don't let all this information sway or scare you from your goal of becoming employed. Keep in mind that you are looking for not just a job, but the right job. And in looking for work in this vein, it is important to realize that even though you are the candidate for employment, those who would hire you are likewise your candidates for being your employer.

To help you remember this fact, here are four qualities that a company should possess before you say "yes" to working there:

• Does it have the correct facilities in house to train you for the coming changes in the work environment? A company that affords opportunities for staff to learn more about computers and is also willing to send you to lectures or seminars on better ways to do business is a company whose eye is on the future and will remain competitive in tomorrow's business world.

• Is the policy of the company to look within its ranks when a high-level position becomes available, or does it look outside the company to fill such slots? You want a company whose motto is to promote from within its own ranks and very seldom hire outside for executive positions.

• Is the salary being offered really exciting to you? If the potential employer offers you a dollar figure, and you truly believe that amount would not compensate you for the work that you would be required to do, reject the offer and keep looking. This is where it's important to have researched your approximate worth in your field and geographic area. (See Chapter 16.)

Many people feel that saying no to a job offer is the worst thing a person can do. They rationalize this idea by telling themselves that even though they have just accepted a lower salary offer than they expected, they will work really hard and prove to their employer that they're worth the extra money. This rationale is baloney. When an employer offers its employees a salary, it's not just telling the potential employee what the job is worth to the employer; it's also showing the financial mindset of the company.

If a company is going to lowball you for your first salary, then every time your salary is going to be reviewed, you will be lowballed. Future raises are nearly always based on a percentage of your current salary. Very few times will an employer change its ways of handling business, especially when it comes to money. Your best bet, when an offer comes to you that is not what you want, is to say no and keep looking.

• Benefits, benefits, benefits. A company that supplies you with health insurance, stock options, vacation and holiday pay, and retirement plans is the one to work for. In today's economy, where Social Security may not be around when you retire and paying for your own health insurance plan is prohibitively expensive, joining a company that offers you a good benefits package is nearly as important as the salary. Being privy to an all-encompassing benefits plan can add extra disposable income to your annual salary.

Negotiating Salary and Benefits

Though the section above tells you something about how to set the salary ball rolling, the critical part comes after the offer has been made. First of all comes the initial salary offer, initial because if you are not reasonably satisfied with the first offer, you will have to negotiate a better number.

One thing to consider about the first salary amount thrown out by the employer in question is how it stacks up in relation to benefits. Benefits packages have changed substantially from the days when your parents were first starting their careers. Twenty to thirty years ago, a young person getting his or her first good job could expect not only a salary, but insurance paid for by the company, a pension plan also paid for in full by the company, and a set vacation period, usually five days the first year, ten the next, and so on. Nowadays, it's anybody's guess.

A typical benefits package today would consist of a salary, a flexible vacation package containing a mixture of fixed vacation time accrued throughout the year and maybe a set number of personal days, insurance benefits paid for in part by the employee, and maybe a retirement savings plan made up in whole or in part by employee contributions. It is important to get the full details on all the components of a benefits package, as well as a rundown of human resources policies. Because many companies can no longer afford to provide the generous package of benefits once given employees, benefits now vary as a way to entice highly qualified workers on board.

If you have multiple offers to consider (and we hope you will), sit down and make a chart of the companies interested in you. (See the accompanying example.) Compare salary, vacation days, retirement savings plans (even though you probably won't still be with the same company by the time you retire, changes in tax and portability laws make the retirement savings package an important factor in your benefits mix), family and maternity leave and child-care policies, profit sharing, equity options, and any other intangibles such as distance to travel to work, parking or commuting costs, and frequency of salary reviews.

Using a chart like this not only will allow you to compare offers for your own sake, but will provide you with information to back you when you call the employer back to negotiate the final package. Saying "I want more money" won't usually work with prospective employers, but informing them of the alternative offers you have

Comparing Job Offers

	ABC Health Care	Xyroxs Health Supply	Managed Care 'R' Us
Salary	$38,000	$40,000	$35,000
Vacation	5 days first year/10 days second year, etc.	5 days first year/7 days second year, etc.	5 days first year/10 days second year, etc.
Retirement Savings	Up to 10% salary/50% employer match	Up to 10% salary/50% employer match, 100% if sales targets met	Up to 7% salary/50% employer match, 75% if sales targets met
Family/ Maternity Leave	2 weeks personal/6 weeks paid maternity	2 weeks personal/6 weeks paid maternity	2 weeks personal/6 weeks paid maternity
Child Care	On-site	None	Off-site, employer paid
Profit Sharing	Year-end bonus based on company sales	Year-end bonus based on department sales	None
Driving Distance/ Parking Costs	2 miles, free	10 miles, $2.00/day	17 miles/public transportation, $3.00/day
Frequency of Salary Review	3 months	6 months	1 year
Misc. Benefits	Closed office with door and good view, cellular phone for business	Company car, frequent national travel, possible international travel	Casual dress, frequent national travel
Abstract	Company growing, possibility for rapid advancement.	Company just entering field, could move fast, could go under in a year or two. Challenging with responsibility, opportunity for on-the-job learning.	Company stable, niche player in market, not very dynamic, safe but unimaginative, not very challenging.

received is likely to make them reconsider their package if they are truly serious about hiring you. Sometimes—especially in smaller companies without rigid personnel policies—you can get a special deal from an employer if you make your case strongly enough.

Looking at the sample chart on page 113, you can see how much easier it is to gauge the value of the total package being offered to you by contending employers if you have the information laid out for you. In addition, a number of the items, such as transportation costs and possibility of travel, may not be taken into consideration by the employer as a "benefit," and things like frequent travel might be a plus or a minus to you. All in all, such direct comparison not only makes you think more clearly about the packages on offer, but gives you something to go by in the future.

Responding to an Offer

Employers often don't have much time to wait for you to make a decision, so it is critical that you respond in a timely manner and be up front with them about other offers that may be on the table. If you expect to hear something from Company B in five to seven days, in most cases you should tell the people at Company A about it, at least so they know what sort of situation you are in.

Letting them know there is someone else interested might make them sweeten the deal as well, though you shouldn't necessarily use this as leverage for that purpose only, because it may backfire. Play it safe and careful in most situations, and prospective employers will likely be understanding.

Once you have reached a decision, you should not only call your interviewer to say that you will accept the position, but you should fax or mail him or her a short note containing your acceptance. And if the employer doesn't offer a written contract, you should request the terms of your employment in writing.

Having these details, such as salary, review frequency, starting date, conditions (such as physical exam, drug testing, non-compete or non-disclosure clauses stating that you will not work for competitors or disclose confidential information), set in concrete from the outset is a good idea. It lets all parties know where they stand and provides you with some goalposts, as well as a clear statement of the conditions of your employment should a dispute arise.

CHAPTER 21

So Where Do I Start Looking?

Finishing school and having your future ahead of you can be a liberating experience. It can also be a stressful one if you don't know where to look for work. Many of us have ideas of what we want to be; we just don't know where those jobs are located. To most of us, our knowledge of the jobs available lies in how many companies we can remember from the advertisements we see on TV, or what billboards we pass on the highways. Few of us realize that there is a wealth of information at our fingertips, if only we knew where to place them.

As discussed in Chapter 16, researching a company is essential when deciding whether you want to apply to work for it. Just as a prospective company tries to find out as much information about you as possible before it hires you, you should be digging up information on it to see if it's the type of organization that you want to work for. Moreover, when you do go into the interview, it would be impressive to have some informed questions about the company to ask the interviewer. Your knowledge of the interviewing firm will impress the person conducting the interview, and will give you an upper hand if a job offer comes your way, because you will know more than even many insiders about how the company operates.

Research materials abound in any public library or even at the local bookstore. What you want to look for is a company's description that seems attractive to you, whether it be the location or the flexibility of the work schedules. What you want is to have the job of your dreams in a company that fits the way you want to do business. The local want ads almost never fulfill that need.

Ron Fry's book *Your First Resume* offers a listing of the following resource books to help you in your job search.

Dun & Bradstreet's Family of Corporate Reference Resources

- *The Million Dollar Directory:* Lists 160,000 companies whose net worth is over $500,000.
- *Top 50,000 Companies:* Lists companies whose net worth is right under $2 million.
- *Business Rankings:* Gives details on the country's top 7,500 companies.
- *Reference Book of Corporate Management/ America's Corporate Leaders:* Offers biographical information of principal officers and directors of the country's top 12,000 firms.

To purchase any of these books or find out where they are located, you can reach Dun & Bradstreet by writing to Dun's Marketing Service, 3 Century Drive, Parsippany, NJ 07054.

Other books that offer information about companies are:

• *Moody's Industrial Manual:* Available by writing to Moody's Investor Service, 99 Church Street, New York, NY 10007.

• *Standard &Poor's Register of Corporations, Directors and Executives*: This book gives you information on 45,000 companies and background listings on more than 70,000 officers. You can get your copy by writing to Standard & Poor's, 25 Broadway, New York, NY 10004.

• *Thomas's Register of American Manufacturing:* Available by writing to Thomas Publishing Company, 1 Penn Plaza, New York, NY 10001.

• *Ward's Business Directory:* This three-volume set includes the listing of 100,000 firms, the majority privately held. Information of this sort is hard to come by, since privately held firms don't have to release to the public much information about their inner workings. These volumes will tell you how many people work for the firms you're interested in and what their annual sales are. It is published by the Information Access Company.

• *The Standard Directory of Advertisers:* Also known as the *Advertiser Red Book,* this publication lists more than 17,000 companies that spend above a certain amount of their annual budgets on advertising and promotion. It details the people who make the advertising decisions for companies.

• *The Fortune 500:* This well-known annual publication is a special issue of *Fortune* magazine. It gives rankings of businesses based on sales.

• *The Oxford Directory of Newsletters:* This publication can be found in many public libraries. It gives you insight into the goings-on of many companies. If you happen to be interviewing with one, it might serve you well to read up on its latest activities.

There are periodicals that can help you find out the state of an industry as well. Surely every business major has already subscribed to *The Wall Street Journal,* just as any public communications student would read *Adweek* magazine. If you don't know the names of the trade magazines in your target field, check out the *Standard Periodical Directory,* published by Oxbridge Communications. You are likely to find not one or two periodicals in your field of interest, but dozens. Call each publication and ask for a recent copy. If you say you are a student, you may get it for free.

When looking at the information on the company where you will be interviewing, it is important to keep some basic questions in mind. You should be continually asking yourself whether this is the right

career for you, whether this company will suit your needs, and whether you will be happy doing the work you'd be paid to do, in the environment you'd be entering.

Here are some other questions that might help you better understand what you are looking for in a company:

- Do you enjoy living in a big city or small town?
- Is a small company with a laid-back feel more your style, or are you looking for the very definition of Corporate America?
- Would a job that had a lot of travel seem exciting to you, or would you rather just drive to work and be in your own bed most nights?
- Are you considering the opportunity to continue your education? Would the company pay for it or allow you to work flexible hours in order to attend class?
- Do you like working on strict deadlines?

These are just a few of the questions that you should be asking yourself as you move along the path toward seeking an employer. It cannot be stressed enough how important it is for you to continually question yourself and the motives behind why you will be choosing one place to work over the other. Answer a lot of questions today, wonder whether the moves you are making are the right ones, because you don't want to find out the hard way that you have made the wrong choice and then have to start all over again.

CHAPTER 22

Should I Take It if They Offer It?

The working world may seem daunting to the uninitiated. You might think that since you're at the bottom of the pecking order, your job choices will be narrow, and that you will have to go to work at any company that will take you. It's a bad idea to think that way. You wouldn't choose a college in that fashion, or even a boyfriend or girlfriend, just because that person was the first to accept you. So don't do it for the early jobs in your career.

You must trust yourself that a satisfactory, if not perfect, work environment is there for you.

In Chapter 21 there were questions you answered about yourself that helped you discover your personal preferences. Now it's time to look at yourself again. But, instead of researching your likes and dislikes, this time you will dig a little deeper: You will uncover what we call your "labor personality." It is important to gain an understanding of how you work and what you expect from others in the work environment. As you know, employers are looking for specific types of personalities when they are interviewing. Learning your type of labor personality not only will help you while you're interviewing, but also will help you gain the maximum fulfillment from your career's work.

We are going to use a model that a large, Midwestern company employs to categorize its employees. According to this company's test, there are four types of characteristics that an employer seeks in a prospective employee. Most likely, the worker will possess all these characteristics, but there is usually one that will dominate.

Listed below are the four general personalities that, based on what job is available, most companies look for in an employee. It is important, while reading the descriptions of the personalities, that you picture yourself doing the job you dream of and how you would like to get that job done. Remember, there are a million ways to accomplish a task. You want to fit yourself into a work environment that appreciates the way you do business. This appreciation will make things easier for you when trying to work with others.

But before we get to the actual personality categories, let's play a little game. Finish the following sentence with the one ending that describes you best:

If I were asked to cut someone's lawn, I would...

A tell the person the price for the job is twenty dollars and that I could do it on Friday (the optimal day for my work schedule).

B let the person know how happy I am to be of service and, between us both, decide when the most optimal time would be to cut the lawn.

C cut the lawn, ask few questions, and accept whatever payment is given.

D take a look at the size of the lawn and the size of the mower's blades, see how many obstacles are in the lawn (i.e., trees, bushes, fallen branches) that would have to be avoided, see how much daylight is left, and see what else I have planned for the day, before accepting the job.

The choice you made reveals something about you. Take a look and see what your choice means.

• *Response A:* Most likely you lean toward handling life's choices with keeping the bottom line in mind. This trait is very important in the world of business. Most leaders in the workplace are bottom-liners. In fact, most leaders would not be nearly as effective if they didn't keep the bottom line at the forefront of their minds.

Some other traits that bottom-liners exhibit are as follows. Being this type of person means you:

Make a decision quickly and usually discuss it with no one
Enjoy immediate gratification
Usually participate in activities where you are in control
Feel that you could do a better job if you were the leader
Don't like being used
Enjoy working in an efficient way

• *Response B:* Your dominant personality trait is being highly sociable or people-oriented. This trait is also very important to the job world. Being strong in the area of interpersonal skills is not only vital to sealing a sales deal, it also is a must for the company's image. There is no company today that will remain successful without its employees knowing how to treat and respect its fellow human beings.

Some other clues to help you decide whether this is your dominant personality would be:

Being well liked by your peers
Loving to gossip and fool around with others
Being spontaneous when it comes to decision making
Enjoying being recognized for your accomplishments
Having an eye for fashion and being considered stylish by your peers
Finding it boring to do anything routine

• *Response C:* Chances are you enjoy following directions. This is by far one of the most important character traits to any company. A company of any size or structure could not maintain order without a staff that follows directions.

To help you decide whether this type of trait dominates your character, check the following. Fitting this description means you:

Are a good listener
Are defined by others as sincere or appreciative
Enjoy the quality of friendship
Like to have others' input on a matter before deciding about it yourself
Feel uneasy when things change suddenly
Don't enjoy being around people who are impatient

• *Response D:* Your dominant personality would be analytic. Without a doubt, this trait is quite vital to a business's operations.

People who fit into this category typically:

Plan every move
Demonstrate a systematic way of thinking
Want to be exact on their predictions; being a hair off is equal to being wrong
Move deliberately when a decision must be made
Enjoy very structured situations
Have a deep pride in their work

Once you have a sense of who you really are, then you can present a fuller package to the employer during the interview. Also, and perhaps more importantly, when the discussion between you and the

company turns to what the duties of the job are, you will know whether you're suited for such work because you will know whether those job qualities match the traits of your dominant personality.

To show how knowing yourself better will only enhance your chances of personal fulfillment on the job site, let's suppose that you're on an interview and the session is going well. You feel that the major you have picked, engineering, is the one for you. Within a few months you will have completed your internship and graduated.

And you also know, having read this chapter, that you're a B-type personality: sociable and people-oriented.

So, during this interview, the conversation turns to the duties that you will be expected to perform: Most of them require your being alone and on the road, driving around Missouri and Nebraska looking for bridges that may have structural problems.

Upon hearing this, a few ideas start to surface in your mind. First, your have a dominant B-type personality (you love to be around others) and there is a part of you that is D (you enjoy highly structured situations). Well, with this job, you will not have much personal interaction, and every day is different from the one before. So, no matter what the salary, you should not accept the job, unless there is a real chance to fulfill yourself later, after you've been promoted. Don't despair about all that education; you might be much happier in an engineering job where you worked with a team of other engineers and architects, for example.

CHAPTER 23

America's Employment Outlook: It's Your Future

Many experts seem to be saying the same thing: On the whole, Generation Xers will enjoy fewer job opportunities than any preceding generation within this century. An article by economist James C. Franklin in the November 1995 issue of the *Monthly Labor Review*, published by the U.S. Department of Labor's Bureau of Labor Statistics (BLS), predicts that from 1994 to 2005, based on moderate market conditions (that means no depression or unexpectedly high inflation within this time frame), total job opportunities will increase by 1.2 percent annually. Put in strict numeric terms, that's 17.7 million more jobs.

Sounds pretty good, doesn't it? All you need is one job, right? And if this prediction is accurate that means there will be about 17,699,999 jobs available for the other job seekers, after you've become secure in your employment niche. So where's the problem?

Here it is, and it's on two interconnected fronts. The first is with the BLS figures prior to 1994. From 1983 to 1994, the BLS reported a 2.0 percent increase in total job growth for this time period; that figure is nearly double what we are experiencing now. Before this time frame the increases in total job growth were even higher. What this trend is telling us is that the demand for an expanding labor force is slowing.

In his book titled *The Great Jobs Ahead* (previously titled *Job Shock*), author Harry S. Dent, Jr., supports the data released by the BLS. He concurs by saying, "Unless you've buried yourself in the world of game-show television, you've seen symptoms of fundamental change in American corporations—layoffs, plant closings, cost cutting and benefit slashing." Dent further states that "even if you read only a little news in 1993, you know the headlines were dominated by stories along the lines of 'Where Did My Job Go?' in *Fortune* magazine and 'Where Did My Career Go? The White-Collar Lament of the 90's' in *U.S. News & World Report*."

In the years since, the focus on job loss has been relentless. It peaked in early 1996 with the presidential candidacy of Republican Patrick Buchanan, who blasted corporate America, and particularly AT&T, for firing tens of thousands of workers. At around this same time, *Newsweek* plastered the picture of AT&T Chairman Bob Allen on its cover, along with other business leaders, and labeled them "Corporate Killers."

I've actually seen this decline in job opportunity within my own family. My mother and I attended the same university, about twenty-five years apart: she in the early '60s and I in the mid-1980s. Her recollection of the function of our school's career placement office is quite different from my own.

In the '60s, the school's gymnasium was converted into a type of convention center. Tables lined the basketball arena and hosted representatives from a wide range of companies. Most of these representatives were from local, in-state firms, but there were some corporations that would venture across state lines and try to recruit students from our alma mater. She remembers the event being similar to a traveling carnival, with all the company reps trying to ring in as many interested prospects as possible. If you had a degree or even a few years of college experience under your belt, most companies dove at the chance to meet you.

This same career placement office operated very differently in the late '80s. Instead of the gymnasium being transformed into a job bonanza, a sheet of paper was placed on the career placement door. It listed the companies that would be interviewing in the coming weeks. There were usually around three or four corporations in a two-week span.

But almost having a college degree was not good enough for most visiting firms; an interviewing student not only had to be secure that graduation was imminent, but also had to possess a certain grade point average (usually a 3.3 or higher) before corporation representatives would even consider talking about working for their company.

—Jay Heflin

The second part of the problem, with the future of work for Generation Xers, deals with the more than 70 million Baby Boomers, people born between 1946 and 1964. These folks not only "tuned in" and "turned on," they also flooded the workforce. Data from the Bureau of Labor Statistics state that the consumers of '60s culture began hitting their sustained peak of entering the workforce back in the early '80s. That dominance will remain constant well into the next century. And what this tidbit of information means to Generation Xers is that there is a huge bottleneck in many career channels throughout the American workplace.

From a practical standpoint, there are too many Baby Boomers holding the jobs to which Generation Xers aspire. People in their thirties and forties have flooded middle management positions—and many of these positions are being eliminated in corporate downsizing.

The table on page 128 compares varying employment needs for major occupational categories during two distinct periods of time: from 1983 through 1994 (actual), and from 1994 through 2005 (projected). As these figures show, there will be a relative slowdown in rate of increase of employment opportunities within certain fields.

So, what is the bottom line to all these percentages? What are the actual jobs that are on the verge of becoming obsolete and therefore should be avoided? What are the actual numbers of jobs soon to be lost in each career? Well, the table on page 129 shows how the BLS projects the future of some jobs, brought on by the changes of a decreased need in the labor force.

Differences in Growth of Major Occupational Categories

Category	Net Increases 1983–1994	Net Increases 1994–2005
Professional specialty	37%	29%
Service	30	23
Technicians	30	20
Marketing and sales	33	18
Executive, administrative, and managerial	35	17
Precision production, craft, and repair	10	6
Operators, fabricators, and laborers	12	4
Administrative support, including clerical	23	4
Agriculture and related	1	-3

Now remember, the declines you see in the table on the next page are not due to economic tides such as depression, recession, or even inflation. What is happening here, in this instance, is the product of progress. When Henry Ford created the automobile assembly line, it revolutionized not only his industry, but all industry. And his improvement was not temporary. This shift toward more efficient production caused many jobs to become obsolete, but it gave rise to jobs that people of his day could not even imagine.

Now we are moving out of the days governed by the industrial revolution; ways of doing business henceforth will be governed more by brain power than by mechanical power. Today we are moving toward a wave of careers that demand creativity and the providing of service, rather than the manufacture of goods.

Dent puts it this way: "The Industrial Revolution put us to sleep in the name of the efficiencies of functional specialization. It forced us to master tasks and to blindly follow standard procedures. In many of us, it diminished the capacity to innovate. It's time to reclaim our most creative, most fulfilling, most human functions."

Occupations With the Largest Projected Numerical Declines, 1994–2005

Occupation	Projected Decrease
Farmers	-273,000
Typists and word processors	-212,000
Bookkeeping, accounting, and auditing clerks	-178,000
Bank tellers	-152,000
Sewing machine operators, garment	-140,000
Cleaners and servants, private household	-108,000
Computer operators, except peripheral equipment	-98,000
Billing, posting, and calculating machine operators	-64,000
Duplicating, mail, and other office machine operators	-56,000
Textile draw-out and winding machine operators and tenders	-47,000
File clerks	-42,000
Freight, stock, and material movers, hand	-36,000
Farm workers	-36,000
Machine tool cutting operators and tenders, metal and plastic	-34,000
Central office operators	-34,000
Central office and PBX installers and repairers	-33,000
Electrical and electronic assemblers	-30,000
Station installers and repairers, telephone	-26,000
Personnel clerks, except payroll and timekeeping	-26,000
Data entry keyers, except composing	-25,000

Of course, the shift to a service-based economy will also have a serious impact on manufacturing. These industries are projected, by the BLS, to lose 1.3 million jobs from 1994 to 2005. Among these will be a loss of 674,000 operator, fabricator, and laborer positions, and a loss of 284,000 precision, production, craft, and repair jobs.

So, what is the future of work? Well, with opportunities in the job market becoming more scarce and more and more people wanting to become a part of the working population, most employers are in a position that could be referred to as a buyer's market: They can afford to be choosy. They can put stiff requirements on prospective employees: like having an A- average in undergraduate school or completing a master's degree. And the reason they can do this is because of this reduced demand in the labor force market.

So securing yourself one of those 17.7 million job openings that are expected to be generated in the future doesn't seem so easy after all, does it? Generation Xers will be expected, by employers, to jump through more hoops and perform more tricks than any other generation before us. Jay's mother's metaphor was right: The job marketplace is like a traveling carnival. Only this time, instead of companies jockeying for our undivided attention, we're all part of the carnival, and the corporations are the guests we wish to entertain.

With all these changes taking place, it is impossible to define exactly what new jobs will be created out of the new innovations of today. What we can predict, with some degree of assurance, is how the jobs currently in existence will fare in the coming century.

Occupations With the Largest Projected Numerical Increases, 1994–2005

Occupation	Projected Increase
Cashiers	+ 562,000
Janitors and cleaners	+ 559,000
Salespersons, retail	+ 532,000
Waiters and waitresses	+ 479,000
Registered nurses	+ 473,000
General managers and top executives	+ 466,000
Systems analysts	+ 445,000
Home health aides	+ 428,000
Guards	+ 415,000
Nursing aides, orderlies, and attendants	+ 387,000
Teachers, secondary school	+ 386,000
Marketing and sales worker supervisors	+ 380,000
Teacher aides and educational assistants	+ 364,000
Receptionists and information clerks	+ 318,000
Truck drivers	+ 271,000
Secretaries, except legal and medical	+ 267,000
Clerical supervisors and managers	+ 261,000
Child care workers	+ 248,000
Maintenance repairers, general utility	+ 231,000
Teachers, elementary	+ 220,000

The BLS projects that twenty occupations will account for nearly half of all the employment growth for the years 1994 through 2005. Of these occupations, jobs related to the retail trade, health care, and education industries seem to be the most frequent in the BLS's top ten jobs between 1994 and 2005. See the table above.

Occupations With the Largest Projected Percentage Increases, 1994–2005

Occupation	Percentage Increase
Personal and home care aides	+ 119%
Home health aides	+ 102
Systems analysts	+ 92
Computer engineers	+ 90
Physical and corrective therapy aides	+ 83
Electric pagination system workers	+ 83
Occupational therapy assistants and aides	+ 82
Physical therapists	+ 80
Residential counselors	+ 76
Human services workers	+ 75
Occupational therapists	+ 72
Manicurists	+ 69
Medical assistants	+ 59
Paralegals	+ 58
Medical records technicians	+ 56
Teachers, special education	+ 53
Amusement and recreation attendants	+ 52
Correction officers	+ 51
Operations research analysts	+ 50
Guards	+ 48

It is interesting to compare the actual number of job increases with the BLS's percentage increases within the same time frame, because they are not the same. See the table above.

One conclusion that can be drawn from the different job categories cited in these two lists is that they are people who provide services, not manufacture products. Also, the fastest-growing professions by percentage are often in emerging industries expected to have major expansions. The fastest-growing professions by sheer number of employees are in fields that are already large, and thereby more stable.

Notice that health care will be a big employer, primarily because the bulk of our population is getting older; by the turn of the century, one out of three people will reach age 50 or older. The mean age will be 39 for the year 2000, as compared to 36 in 1990.

After all this information about changes in careers, increases in the qualifications for existing jobs, and the net effects of jobs becoming obsolete, you are probably becoming curious as to what is out there for you. More importantly, you're probably interested in not only what you will be doing, but how much money you'll be making. For in truth, you're not seeking to get hired just for the sport of it; you need the cash!

To satisfy this curiosity, listed below are several jobs with projected salary earnings for the year 2000. These projections are from Carol Kleiman's book *The 100 Best Jobs for the 1990s and Beyond*. Please keep in mind, the salaries listed in the table below are in dollars not adjusted for inflation.

With advanced education and multiple skills becoming increasingly important, salaries will certainly reflect this change; skilled people will be well paid for the work they're doing. The estimated average income for the turn of the century worker varies with every expert, but the annual income usually falls somewhere in the vicinity of $35,000.

Projected Salary for Certain Jobs in the Year 2000

Job	Salary
Retail salesperson	$20,000 to $27,000
Registered nurse	$50,000 (starting)
Computer system analyst	$48,000 to $67,000
Home health aide	$20,000
Licensed practical nurse	$42,000
Teacher	$46,733
Professor	$71,211
Secretary/office administrator	$24,000
Truck driver	$24,000 to $35,000
Clerical/office supervisor	$24,000
Office/business machine repairer	$37,565

CHAPTER 24

Computers Revolutionize the Workplace

As you might have guessed, the big push that is leading today's revolution is the computer. Ironically, at the computer's inception, some experts thought only a few machines would be needed to fulfill the country's computing responsibilities. As Julie Kling Burns states in her book *Opportunities in Computer Systems Careers*:

> The phenomenal growth in the number of computer systems reflects their growing importance in almost every aspect of life. In 1947, computer engineer Howard Aiken predicted that six computers would satisfy the computing needs of the United States. By 1955, there were 244 computer systems in use, and by 1980 this number had increased to over 600,000. In 1984, businesses and individuals in the United States purchased over two million computers. By 1994, worldwide shipments of personal computers and workstations were over 47 million.

Aiken clearly underestimated just how valuable the computer really would be—and how much it would change the workplace. In fact, many jobs that were once done by people are now done almost entirely by computers, and jobs have been lost as a result.

Now, some may think the loss of jobs to overseas competitors is also a major contributing factor as to why certain jobs are shrinking in the United States, but as William Bridges states in his book, *Job Shift*:

> Ten years ago it was common to blame our job problems on overseas competition. However, many organizations are insulated from overseas competition, so that answer is clearly inadequate [to why jobs are being lost today]. Even in cases where jobs have been lost because goods can be made more cheaply overseas, the story is more complicated than we usually realize. When we talk about jobs going overseas, we're likely to leave out a very important part of the story: production leaves these shores, not jobs per se. For every one thousand American jobs lost in such a relocation, as few as a hundred may be gained by the overseas country that wins the relocation production facility.
>
> Jobs do not follow the old physics principle of conservation of matter, where nothing ever disappears absolutely. Job loss is not a zero-sum game, where they win and we lose, because relocation is appealing only partly because pay is lower for the same job in Malaysia or Mexico than in the United States. An increasingly important factor in relocation is that it is easier to start from scratch in a location where people's attitudes are not compromised by decades of experience with traditional industrialism—and, of course, with jobs.

What Bridges is saying is that it is easier for a company to apply new technological advances to business in a country where most people have no or little concept of how business is done. In the United States, if a company were to impose layoffs because of a newfound technology, most people would protest. But in Mexico, where people are not accustomed to working with this technology, a company can set up its newfound toy and hire as few people as it needs to run the thing—all with the applause (and no protesting) from the local government and the townspeople. This is pretty hard-core, but unfortunately it is how the real world operates.

But no matter what the ethics are of some corporations, benefits from the newfound revolution will abound within our own borders as well; remember, the United States of America isn't called the land of opportunity for nothing. Prosperity is something we're known for around the world. That will not change so fast.

As stated earlier, today's revolution is due to the advances made with the computer. What used to be considered a hobby toy of nerdy introverts a few years ago is now the standard operating tool for almost all enterprises, large and small.

So, what are some of the ways computers are revolutionizing the workplace and our way of living? Harry S. Dent, Jr., author of not only *The Great Jobs Ahead,* but also *The Great Boom Ahead,* describes what is happening in the workplace as "job shock"; it's the wake-up call for the new revolution. One day a person rises from bed and, without warning, his or her job is gone.

This revolution should not be considered a radical change, but more of an evolution. Some flowering plants appear to burst into bloom in just a few days, so that to the eye it seems as if the plant was dormant for the preceeding months. But actually, within its buds, the plant was hard at work, with each flower growing its way toward maturity ever since the winter's thaw.

This same idea goes for computers. Professionals have been working on perfecting the machines for more than fifty years; it just so happens that now is the time that the use of computers is coming into full bloom. What Dent views as sudden has actually been creeping along. It's only recently that most of the population has been affected by it so pervasively.

So what is happening to the workplace while the computers are blooming? Plenty. Dent sees the workplace changing in two broad ways.

One: Computers Are the New Office Worker

At their inception, computers only added to the paper-shuffling problem. High-speed printers could churn out mountains of information; too bad no one knew what to do with it all. Instead of computers reaching and exceeding their potential, often they just sat on top of desks, being as productive as any other paperweight.

But times did change. Today, instead of computers adding to the amount of bureaucracy within a company, they are eliminating it. Computers are now responsible for the repetitive work done in the office. The computer handles chores like accounting calculations or sales information that need to be updated time and time again throughout a business week or even day.

The computer has become so effective at mastering some office tasks that it has been replacing some of the office workers who used to be in charge of those tasks. As Dent says, "New computers are finally being used to replace bureaucrats and middle managers instead of to make them more efficient. That's what's driving job shock." Computers have become the new breed of white-collar worker.

William Bridges supports Dent's observation. Bridges sees the computer's powers becoming more prevalent within the work arena. In coining a word, to "informate," he describes the way technology is being used on today's and tomorrow's jobs. States Bridges:

> The verb "to informate" describes the way data is inserted between the worker and the product. The factory worker no longer manipulates the sheet of steel; he [now] manipulates the data about the steel. Work that has been informated is no longer physical but is, instead, a sequence or pattern of information that can be handled and changed almost as if it were tangible. An order, once entered into a salesperson's laptop in a customer's office, becomes simply data, and it automatically triggers a chain of data events with a minimum of further human intervention.

Bridges cites an example to further illustrate what he is saying: "Mazda Motors had informated its account-payable system [and] woke Ford Motor Company up to its possible savings. Mazda, which is admittedly a good deal smaller than Ford, did with five—yes five—employees what Ford was using four hundred to accomplish. Obviously, informated work needs fewer people."

Will this reign continue? Most likely it will, because of the next factor Harry Dent sees with computers and the future of the workplace.

■ Two: Computers Are on the Brink of Unthinkable Power

Recall seeing on TV back in the late '60s and early '70s computers dealing with the space program or other technical governmental endeavors? Remember those huge rooms with those monsterlike machines lining the walls? And hordes of goofy men wearing horned-rimmed glasses with greasy-looking hair, running up and down the length of those big machines, caring for them as though they were infants? Those rather large devices were state-of-the-art computers back then. Nowadays that same power—or even more—can be produced with a mechanism no larger than a man's wallet, and it will be far more user-friendly.

As George Gilder, author of the book *Microcosm*, says, "With the predictable progress of information technologies we can project that within a decade we will see the power of sixteen Cray supercomputers on a single microchip that cost less than one hundred dollars."

With all this new technology permeating the workplace, it would be foolish to believe that the lifestyles at home would remain unchanged; computers in the office are only the first stop. Life away from the office is already being transformed by the computer age as well. Dent sees the new revolution happening on three fronts. Of course, these innovations will first arrive in the office, but soon the home will benefit from them as well.

● Front One: The Smart Card

Imagine having a credit-card-size computer that will allow you access to your company's billing reports, client sales history, or amount of vacation days you have accumulated, and retrieving this information at any ATM-like machine, anywhere in the country. Equipped with a microchip for memory, the smart card will eliminate delays in renting an automobile, getting flight information, or purchasing Super Bowl tickets.This card could also replace the wallet and still hold the family pictures that it once carried.

● Front Two: The Smart Phone

With fewer people in the workplace, those who remain will need to be mobile. Having a smart cellular phone will enable employees this freedom to fax, send, and retrieve messages and to scan data. All the tasks they need to accomplish will be accomplished through the smart phone—even writing letters.

As Dent states, "Beginning in 1996 when Motorola's first low-orbit satellites are in operation, continuing into 2001 when Microsoft and McCaw plan to have a broader network of such satellites in orbit, the smart phone will permit everybody to access a global, wireless network."

Front Three: The Smart Television

Kids of today and tomorrow will no longer be running home, after school, to catch the series of reruns playing on the television set the way we Generation Xers did when we were younger. Nowadays, children will have at their fingertips (literally, considering the TV set is run by the remote control) scores of learning, movie, and communication channels.

But this invention will not only benefit the younger folks in a family. Fiber-optic cables will also plug the household workers into network databases, sales meetings across the globe or in the home office, library sources for research on particular office projects, and a whole host of other areas too numerous to enumerate within these pages. The television will soon lose its nickname "the idiot box" and will be considered an invaluable source of information.

There's no mistaking that computers are an ever-present factor in the way business is conducted and will be conducted in the future. But why have these machines become so powerful and popular? Why is the idea of eliminating human employees becoming an increasingly viable notion? Why don't we pull the plug on these computers and keep doing business the usual way?

The answer is simple: progress. Business was conceived on this notion of progress. For Corporate America to resist this change would be a strike against its very nature. Computers don't call in sick and never need a vacation (or even a coffee break, for that matter). Computers don't go on strike for higher wages or better working conditions. What has spurred the revolution is the corporate need to be better, faster, stronger—qualities that make up the winning side to any firm's bottom line.

As a final note to this section, there is one place in a company's hierarchy that the computer will never overtake: the top echelon. CEOs or business owners will never be in a position of becoming obsolete. The reason is that somebody has to power up the computer and tell it what to work on. Decisions about what a company is doing for business must be made before the computer can be turned on—unless what the computer experts are saying about artificial intelligence turns out to be true!

Changes in Jobs Within the New Work Environment

Now that you understand this new revolution, it is time to see how the workplace will be affected by these changes. In her book, *The 100 Best Jobs for the 1990s and Beyond*, Carol Kleiman, a nationally syndicated business columnist, sees the workplace changing in the following ways:

- *Decentralization of the office.* Coworkers who used to sit in the next cubicle might be in factories on the other side of the world or working out of their homes. Instant telecommunications and automation are linking the employees and allowing them to work as one.
- *Employees independently governed.* Instead of the typical hierarchy of command, where the boss instructs the employee on how to accomplish a certain task, the emphasis will be on hiring highly educated, skilled

workers who can think for themselves. These people might be employees of the company or working as freelancers. Either way, they will be responsible for more of the decision-making process that drives the job being executed.

• *College and graduate degrees becoming mandatory.* Liberal arts majors will be heavily recruited as opposed to the business grads who were so popular in the past. Also, a growing knowledge of topics such as computers, mathematics, and interpersonal skills will be needed. Remember, workers of tomorrow will not only be responsible for getting just one aspect of a job done, they will undertake many tasks, including decisions about the product and its promotion.

• *Flexible work hours.* With the growing emphasis on spending quality time with families and having a work style that coexists with the needs of home, most companies will not adhere to the traditional nine-to-five office hours pattern. Most workers will make their own schedules for completing a project and spending free time with friends and families. But don't let this freedom fool you; most predictions say the old forty-hour work week will increase to sixty.

• *Increases in wellness programs.* Because recruiting and training employees will become ever more expensive, many companies will ill afford to lose an employee once he or she has been fully trained. To keep personnel on board, large employers are doing all they can to combat the common problems workers face, such as addictions, illnesses, or family traumas. This means that firms will increasingly offer a wide variety of wellness programs to their employees.

• *Diminished union power.* Since many companies in the manufacturing sector will employ fewer and fewer employees, unions will become less powerful. As Kleiman states, "Only 16% [of today's working population are] union members, continuing a steady drop from more than 30% in 1970."

CHAPTER 25

The Golden Rule(s) of the Office

No matter what field of expertise people choose, there are universal skills that all of them need to get their job done. These are people skills. Some of you might think that just because you are not going into sales or aren't planning to deal with the public firsthand, you don't need people skills. Well, you do.

Even if your job is 100 percent technical, you will have to deal with people. No one, not even someone who works alone at home, can evade conversing with people to get the job done. Think about it: Even calling to reorder some office supplies involves dealing with another person, and doing it correctly requires the right people skills.

Some industry experts might tell you that the people skills you use with your boss are different from the ones you use with your working peers. Don't listen to them. Even though there is a hierarchy in the corporate world and you must answer to some and give orders to others, each person is human and deserves to be treated the same way. If you've ever had a boss who treated you like a second-class citizen, you know how demeaning that experience can be, not to mention how it affects your personal production. Treating everyone with respect, the way you wish to be treated, will not only give you a good feeling inside, it will make you more fun to work with—something that will get you noticed in the most positive sense by the bosses.

But what about when a person is not treating you with the same respect that you are showing him or her? That is still no reason to fly off the handle and start behaving like that person. Everyone knows that it is not easy to remain calm in situations like this, but if you follow the Golden Rule—do unto others as you would have them do unto you—it will serve as a guide for you and possibly stop the person who is being so disrespectful from acting so ungraciously.

Following the Golden Rule is challenging. When work situations get tense and the office begins to feel like a pressure cooker, the first thing that tends to get tossed out the window is the Golden Rule. What people should do when things get hot is cool them off as quickly as possible and restore civility.

To combat these situations, and to reinforce the Golden Rule, some tips are listed below that can help you defuse a tough situation and still keep everyone's self-respect intact. (These are adapted from Bradley Richardson's book *Jobsmarts for Twentysomethings*.) Remember, these tips are not prescribed just to help you with your boss, your client, or your coworkers. They are here to help you with all of them. Because, behind all the titles and all the politics, we're all just people.

The Golden Rules of the Office

- *Think of the other person's needs.* Before you meet with someone, whether that person is a client or a colleague in your company, try to consider the way he or she might be thinking, and present what you want to say in a form that will meet that person's needs.

  Let's say you're at your first job and, as with a lot of first jobs, you are in charge of tasks no one wants, such as moving some office furniture around. Moving furniture is about the most disruptive thing a person can do in an office. It blows the concentration of everyone who happens to be in the area.

  Now, knowing this, you might want to warn those people affected by the disruption that a huge desk is coming through the office in about an hour, and that perhaps then it would be a good time for them to take lunch or not to make any important phone calls. The people to whom you are saying this will not be happy about the disruption, but they will appreciate being notified.

- *Respect everyone's time.* When you are meeting with your boss or conversing with clients, be straightforward. Most people have the fleeting attention span of Homer Simpson. If you haven't grabbed their attention in a few seconds, you probably won't ever get it. To ensure that you have their undivided attention, say right off the bat what is on your mind.

Do not start the conversation with the details of what steps you took to reach your conclusion. Get to the conclusion as soon as you begin talking. If the client or the boss would like more information, let him or her decide that and ask you for the details.

Also, if the matter that you are presenting to your coworkers or client is large and time-consuming, instruct them of this fact. Give them the option of hearing the bottom line now or setting up a meeting in the near future to address the matter. And, when giving this latter option, make sure you are prepared with times and dates that already fit into your schedule.

Remember, everyone has an agenda for the day. Some people, like managers or clients, may not have much time to hear your story. Telling them right up front will allow them the freedom to hear more about your situation or take your bottom-line assessment and go on about their day. Using this quick-and-dirty approach allows you to respect their time and accomplish what you want to get done.

• *Communicate to others what your needs are.* It doesn't matter whether you're dealing with a subordinate, a superior, or a client. People want to know why you are talking to them. This idea goes beyond being straightforward on a specific subject. It's letting people know who you are and why you desire to include them. For example, let a subordinate know that you value an employee who is on time for meetings. Let your boss know about your career plans and what you would like to see in your future. Let clients know how important it is that you understand all their needs so that you can truly accommodate them.

Putting this tip into practice allows people to see more of you than your work. It also builds a trust between you and others; people feel much more comfortable around others whom they understand. Opening yourself up allows others to do the same, and is the basis of the best business relationships; people like working with those whom they consider to be a friend.

• *Treat everyone like a client.* It doesn't matter whether it's the mailroom attendant or the CEO. When you pass that person in the hall, say "good morning" and smile. Acknowledging a person's presence is one of the best ways to compliment him or her.

Also, for you salespeople out there, when approaching the receptionist or your client's assistant, remember that they are the client as well. Many times, when it comes to buying a product, the decision maker will ask members of the support staff which product they think will serve the office best. It doesn't hurt for that support staff to think of you as a nice person when deciding which product the company should purchase. Remember that selling is a numbers game, and anything you can do to increase your odds—even the smallest things—can mean an edge over a competitor.

• *Have an undefined job description.* Have you ever asked for help while working, only to be told "it's not my job"? Isn't that frustrating? If you plan to get it together by 30, you just can't be one of those people who does only what they are specifically required to do. Successful people know that this "I don't do windows" mentality went out the window a long time ago.

It's impossible for the employer who hires you to know exactly what your job will entail, especially for an entry-level position. One day you could be assisting the boss with a sales meeting, the next day you could be calling past-due debtors asking when the check is going to arrive. Be open to all of it. That is how you learn the business and become known as a person who becomes indispensable.

One time, a friend of mine who was working as an intern at an advertising agency was asked to move some boxes for a person who was not his boss or was not even from his department. My friend denied the request, and the person, who was an officer of the firm, had to move the boxes herself. Now, my friend was hoping for a full-time job from this firm after graduation. Needless to say, he wasn't offered it, and he couldn't figure out why.

In his defense, he is not lazy. In fact, he's a hard worker, but he was naive about how the business world operates. He truly thought that by moving the boxes he was taking someone else's job away, and it would make that person look bad in the eyes of the employer. What he failed to see was that a superior asked him to do a job and that he was obliged to do it. When he denied the request, it only looked bad for him, not for the person whose job it actually was to move the boxes.

—Jay Heflin

• *Be responsible for your work.* This tip ties in closely to the one above. If you tell your boss or one of your clients that a project will be done by Friday at 3:30, it had better be done. No one likes to wait for something beyond its deadline.

Also, and more importantly, sometimes you may not see how your job fits into the whole scheme of things, and think that being late will not have consequences for others. Don't deceive yourself. Your boring data entry job may seem unimportant standing alone. But put in the context of getting a direct mail campaign under way in time for the Christmas selling season, the project appears a whole lot different.

Bottom line: If you said your work would be done by Friday at 3:30, keep your promise. Employers rarely forget when a person fails to meet a deadline, and they hardly ever give that person a second chance with an equally important project. If you fail with your first deadline, chances are your next project will not be as vital to the company as the first one was—and you can probably forget about that promotion you wanted.

• *Suggest answers to any problems you bring up.* One of the best things you can do to impress colleagues is offer solutions to problems that they didn't know existed. Doing this gives you the ability to accomplish two things simultaneously: display your intelligence and relieve people of worry.

No one likes to hear details of how the wheels of industry—particularly their own business—are going to grind to a halt if something isn't done. What they are willing to listen to is how something needs to be done and how you propose to do it. Remember, though, that when you have a suggestion on how to fix a system, it is crucial that you clear this suggestion with any superiors. You don't want to unknowingly cause more headaches while trying to repair a problem.

• *Be responsible for your actions and those of your subordinates.* Corporate America, by sheer design, is a breeding ground for passing the buck. The subordinates blame the superiors, who blame the officers, who blame those invisible people known as the stockholders. Don't get caught up in this frenzy if you can possibly avoid it. It's easy for a superior to know when you've fouled up. Accept it and its consequences, and move on.

It is inevitable that there will be bumps, large and small, along the path of your career. No one escapes the flaw of human error. The important thing to do, when you err, is to take responsibility for it.

I have always hated starting a new job. The first week I always put too much pressure on myself, and I never know whether I'm doing the right things or not. You've probably felt the same way.

However, having had four different employers since graduating from college, I've learned how to make these early weeks in any job somewhat more tolerable. What I do is acknowledge, before showing up for work the first week, that the first several days of work are going to be miserable. But also, I acknowledge that as a new employee, my boss is going to cut me some slack I won't get later.

If you can ready yourself for the likely discomfort of a new job before ever showing up, at the end of the first week it won't seem as bad as it might have.

—Richard Thau

No one can deny your integrity when you do this. Not accepting responsibility is the only way to make a bad situation worse.

• *Avoid office gossip at all cost.* Most people who are the target of office gossip feel that it is a form of backstabbing. It is.

The best policy to have, when you are in a group and the conversation turns to gossip, is to walk away and get back to work. Most people won't even notice that you are gone because they are so focused on the subject of the gossip.

Keep in mind that being caught gossiping, particularly by the subject of your gossip, can be one of the most embarrassing moments of your life. Not only do you have to think of something quick to rationalize why you are talking in an unflattering way about the person who just walked into the room, you also have to apologize profusely so that you can reestablish a normal working relationship. It can be quite difficult, particularly if the person is sensitive about being talked about.

• *Go directly to the source when you disagree with something.* Many times during your professional career, situations will arise that make you uncomfortable. It could be a company policy that you see as unfair, or it just might be the way your boss is treating you. No matter what the case, go directly to the source and tell the person how you honestly feel.

Failing to do this and going to that person's superior will look like backstabbing and make you a focus of negative attention in the office. In fact, if you do go to the superior, the first thing the superior will ask you is whether you have discussed this grievance with the person in question first. Saying "no" will tell that person a lot about your character.

There is a big exception to this rule, which you can probably guess. If the grievance you have with the other employee involves something of a criminal nature and you could get hurt if you confronted that person, then it is best that you go to the superior. There should be no reason for you to put yourself in danger working for a company, no matter how much it is paying you.

• *Take advice from everyone, not just your superiors.* There is no greater fool than one who believes everything a superior says and nothing that a subordinate says. The hierarchy that exists when you show up

is bound to change: Remember this! Your flunky one day could be your boss the next, and if you had listened to him when he was below you in the pecking order, he might not be above you now.

Taking advice also works well with clients. Not only are they the ones who probably know your product or service as well as you do, but they could teach you a few things. It's true, as the saying goes, that "everybody's a critic." But some critics know what they're talking about and can be particularly useful if they're constructive in their criticism.

- *Never take someone for granted.* This tip applies to clients as well as your corporate peers and subordinates. Many times, once a client becomes a dependable and regular source of revenue, the sales staff begin to set their sights on other game. Although this is fully understandable, you have to keep in mind that these regular clients are still spending their hard-earned dough on your product and still deserve the attention and respect they received when they first walked in the door.

As for taking a colleague for granted, that is another story. Many people who work together for a long period of time come to think of each other as family. And families are notorious for taking each other for granted. You can always depend on one of the office staffers, for example, to take out your trash, just as it was Mom's job to make dinner every night. Well, think about how much Mom appreciated it when, one night, you said, "thank you" to her for the dinner she made. That is exactly how people in the office will feel when you thank them for doing their job. Everyone knows that the reason the guy takes your trash is because he's getting paid for it, but that is still no reason that his efforts should go unnoticed.

Using these tips will help you gain the respect of everyone you come into contact with in your professional life. Treating others as you would like others to treat you will have a tremendous effect on your productivity. Potential clients won't dodge your phone calls or office visits. Bosses will listen to you, even when busy, because they will understand that if you are telling them something, it must be important. And working with your peers will be more enjoyable because the relationship will be one made out of respect and not trying to outdo each other for a possible promotion.

It would be naive to think that every person you will be working for, or with, will treat you in exactly the same way that has just been described. Let's get real: Many people will not be acting in the respectful fashion that we recommend for you. In fact, some of your coworkers might be downright deceitful and try to steal all or part of your well-earned credit, just so they can wave those accomplishments in a superior's face, in the hope of receiving a promotion.

Just because there are people like that in the workplace doesn't mean that it is OK for you to act in the same fashion. Superiors usually have a sense of a subordinate's morals and will factor that understanding into their thought process when considering the employee for a promotion or work assignment.

But let's say that a fellow worker does steal the spotlight from you on a job and you feel that it's unjust for the boss to congratulate him or her for the work you did. How can you go to the boss and prove that that person lied? Well, you must do it carefully, and only when you can prove it beyond a doubt. (You don't want people misconstruing you as petty if you complain without good evidence.)

The way you do this is through documentation. If you fear someone is going to steal your thunder, write down every task you completed to get a project done, including the names of people with whom you spoke. Having proof of your work will allow you to show your bosses that the work completed was honestly yours.

But one final caveat: You have to pick your battles. Don't get all bent out of shape every time someone shows you up, even if it's unjustified. Your boss hates to resolve disputes between employees, so don't make a big deal out of every slight.

CHAPTER 26

How to Prevent Work From Overtaking Your Sanity

If you thought juggling all your school responsibilities was hard, just wait. Today's professionals are spending more and more time at their jobs. Most used to view forty hours of work a week a full workload. Now it seems that the normal work week lasts about sixty hours, possibly eighty in some professions such as law and accounting.

Right now, if you're still in school, it might be hard to imagine having a job that would keep you so busy. But you must remember, the most fulfilling jobs are almost never the ones where you just show up to work at 9:00 in the morning, take your one-hour lunch break religiously at 12:30, and leave for home at 5:00, no matter how much work you have to complete. And these are never the jobs that position you to get it together by 30. For the professional immersed in what he or she is doing, it is commonplace to lose track of time and stay as long as necessary in order to get the job done.

Even if they love their work, many people complain that it is impossible to have it all: a fulfilling career, a family, a home, hobbies, and so on. And they're justified in feeling that way. The demands that work places on us are often overwhelming and squeeze out the other parts of our life that we enjoy most. But there are ways to cope, especially if you develop good habits early on.

The following steps, some adapted from Bradley Richardson's *Jobsmarts for Twentysomethings*, won't solve all the conflicts that are bound to arise as you work toward building a meaningful career. It is possible, however, to plan wisely so as to prevent unnecessary pressures that complicate your life.

• *Keep the "urgent versus important" distinction straight.* This has got to be one of the biggest problems people face; they confuse what's urgent with what's important. Think about all the things that a typical person in an office is asked to do. How many of them appear urgent? Plenty. But how many of them could have been put off because they were not really important? Plenty, too. And how many important things that really should have been completed long ago never were completed because they were not urgent?

When faced with two competing tasks, ask yourself which one—if not completed soon—would create the more drastic consequences for you down the road. This way you'll know what to do next. Repeating this process will prove quite educational, since it will illustrate how much time you spend doing things that really should not be done by you ever, let alone in a rush.

Here's an example. You're at your desk and your friend calls to say that he's up for a new job and he has just updated his resume, and he needs someone to look it over right away. "Would you do it?" he asks. "Of course," you say, "fax it right over." But then you realize you've been thinking of changing jobs for a while yourself, and have never gone out to buy that resume guidebook you've been thinking about for months. How many times have you put off buying that book because of something more urgent that's arisen? What's more important, your career or a series of urgent tasks, which, after you've done most of them, you can't even remember?

• *Set realistic goals.* Any of us can say that we want to be president of the United States when we grow up. It is a different thing to do it. What most successful people do is allow their hearts to tell them what they wish to become, and allow their minds to chart their progress toward that dream. A common error with most people who fail at attaining their dreams is a lack of realism and inability to focus.

Let's take the biggest, toughest dream, being President of the United States, as an example, since it makes the point well. If this is your dream, you need to be looking at your *next* step today. Preparing your nomination speech before a major political convention is not the wisest use of your time.

What you should be doing, depending on where you are along the path of this dream, is finding out what you can do to move yourself closer to the political arena. Is it running for a position in your school's government? Could it be volunteering your services to help your community? Or are you ready for college and thinking about having political science as your major in school? The most important item in attaining any goal is to make that goal realistic. And a realistic goal is one that proceeds step by step, taking one day at a time, not wondering about how to jump over hypothetical hurdles that may or may not occur years down the road.

• *Get a good sense of how long a project should take you.* When you are assigned a project on the job, it is crucial to calculate the duration of that project and how its schedule fits the rest of your schedule. A good way to decipher how much time a project will take is to look at it not in its entirety, but rather in bits and pieces. And be conservative with your time estimates; things have a way of taking longer than planned.

Dividing a project into smaller jobs will help you better understand how long the whole process will take. If you've been asked to orchestrate a direct mail campaign from start to finish, the best way to find out when the piece will be ready to hit the post office is to break the job down. How long will it take to design the mailing pieces? How long will the printing of the pieces take? How long will it take to get the correct mailing list ready from the direct mail company? How long will transportation of the pieces take, going from step to step? Arriving at the answers to these questions will help you better understand the time frame involved in this job.

Now, being new to a company and wanting to impress everyone might inspire you to take on a task for which you don't have time. If you do choose to head a project that will keep you in the office way past midnight for a few weeks, just remember, the job had better be done on time and done right. No superior will take into consideration the effort you put forward if in the end the job was done incorrectly.

• *Stay on schedule.* After you have planned out your week, stick to it. View your schedule as your personal time bible. If you are supposed to be in a meeting at 2:00 and you have not yet accomplished what you wanted to achieve by then, stop your work and go to your 2:00 appointment. When you return, figure out what additional time you need to finish the earlier task. But under no circumstances let the fact that the task is running overtime throw your schedule off for the rest of the day.

Also, get a specific answer from people if you need to set up a meeting or conference. Having them say, "we'll talk later" won't help you acquire what you need from them. Gently pin them down on a time to meet, one that fits with your schedule and theirs.

The most important item to consider when figuring out a time to meet is when that meeting would be most beneficial to you in getting your project completed. Let's take the direct mail project cited earlier. If you need to meet with the local postmaster about setting up a time for the U.S. Postal Service to pick up your mailing pieces, because the pieces need to be mailed by a certain date, be sure to remind the postmaster of that fact. People who face regular deadlines will respect the fact that you have one too and will often try to accommodate you.

• *Know when to pass work off to subordinates.* Any good manager has to know when to give work to a colleague in order to get the job done. Most people, when they enter managerial status—which may be your goal if you're reading this book—have a hard time with delegation. They don't want to bother others by giving them more work. But you must remember that these subordinates are being paid to do the work that you assign them. Besides, you can't do a whole job by yourself.

Just as it is important to delegate, it is equally important how you delegate. Keep in mind that many adults don't like to be told what they have to do. Even though this is your job, it must be done with-

out stepping on any tender egos. To avoid hurting people's feelings, it is always a good idea to ask them whether they could handle the task you have in store for them.

Once they have agreed to the task, it is up to you to give them all the information they need to complete the job correctly. Saying, "Here you go," and handing them a stack of papers is not the best way of communicating what you need them to do. Schedule a meeting so that the two of you can discuss what needs to be done.

After the meeting, you must allow your employees to do the task in the best way they see fit. Trust them. If you see them calling a direct mail broker before you would have chosen to, don't interrupt their conversation and start dictating how the job should be done. You must allow them to think for themselves. If you are really worried about whether this employee will make sufficient progress, set up periodical meetings to help gauge their progress.

- *Be efficient with your free time.* This is not to suggest that you work on your office projects during your weekends or on vacation. (Although, sadly enough, you probably will—at least sometimes during your weekends.) Rather, look at those moments of your day when you have fifteen minutes to kill and see what you can do productively with them.

Just because you are done with the day's business at the office doesn't mean you should stop thinking about the office. Little moments like waiting for your train or sitting in stopped traffic are hidden moments of opportunity. Now would be a good time to recheck tomorrow's schedule. Did you forget to set anything up? Are you working efficiently? Did what you accomplish today set you up to start tomorrow's schedule right away?

Using these little gaps of time, ones that aren't really leisure and aren't really office hours, can help you clear up details that will help you run things more smoothly once you are back in the office. They also can relieve your mind of thinking about the office once you have arrived home, a time that should be spent enjoying your family and friends.

Causes of Poor Time Management

Sometimes more can be learned on how to do something correctly by seeing how it is done incorrectly. In his book, Richardson lists a few examples of how a person can poorly manage work time:

- Working without a plan or list
- Not delegating
- Trying to perfect every detail when possibly that item shouldn't have had so much time spent on it
- Failing to control interruptions
- Refusing to say no to anything, like taking on another project or getting a beer after work, when work should be your first priority
- Not stopping to think and see how your plan is coming along and what adjustments need to be made to better its progress

CHAPTER 27

The Art of Self-Promotion

In the workplace, you are going to find two types of people: those who take charge of their careers and those who let others do it for them. There's no way to get it together by 30 if you let someone else control your fate.

Keep in mind that if you are to master your own destiny, people have to know what you've achieved (this means your bosses). There's no point in doing something great in the office if you're the only person who knows about it. So don't be shy about getting out the word about your successes. But keep in mind: You're going to find yourself walking that fine line between being respected for your achievements and being disliked for your boastfulness. So don't gloat. Just quietly get the word out.

There are a few ways to put yourself in the position to achieve a good reputation in the workplace, and the following advice should be applicable to your situation. If it isn't, you'll find a way to alter it so that it becomes so.

• *Take on a risky project.* "To boldly go where no man has gone before," said Captain James T. Kirk of the U.S.S. Enterprise. Heed his advice, and agree to a project that most people in the office would be fearful of trying. Once you have proved yourself on a few projects that didn't require much risk, it's time to accept one of the more high-profile jobs that involve a greater chance of failure.

When you take on a project like this, be sure to give it your all. But know that if you succeed, you'll be hailed as a leader and hero in the office. If you fail, well, no one expected you to be successful anyway, since the odds were against you.

• *Take a position.* In too many meetings, when people are asked for their opinions, they try to sound neutral. They come off saying things you would expect to hear from a politician during an election year, nothing concrete. Contrary to politics, no one likes a "yes" man licking their boot heels. The people who display this type of office politics are usually the least respected in everyone's mind.

Business can't run this way. If you say what is on your mind you will be noticed for having a backbone—particularly if you are thoughtful and not destructive in your comments. Also, if your superior happens to disagree with your opinion, don't argue about it in the meeting. It will only take up the other's time. Instead, meet with that superior on your own time and ask him or her to explain to you why you were wrong. This action will help you understand more of the business and get you noticed as a person who not only has a backbone, but also is eager to learn. Employers like seeing both those aspects in the people they promote.

• *Become an expert.* If there is a need in the office and you are the person who knows the most about it, you will become noticed quickly.

Two rules apply when deciding in which areas to become expert. One is that you have to like it to know much about it. Personal interest is the best motivator for understanding something from the

ground up. If you enjoy your area of expertise, you'll be able to help your co-workers even more than you probably realize.

The other rule is to pick an expertise that will remain useful indefinitely. If you're working in a rapidly changing industry, think strategically how your becoming expert in a certain field will not only help the company in the present, but be useful two years hence.

My brother-in-law, who is an attorney, was telling me about a business trip he recently took where his firm called in forensic accountants to help them with a case. I, of course, wanted to know what forensic accountants are.

He explained that they are people who have training in not only accounting, but also criminal investigations. Not only do they know double-entry bookkeeping, but they can also check the fingerprints on the ledger.

And as he told me about this field, my first thought was something my father's friend once said to me years ago: The most successful people are typically those who master not one field, but two, and in the process fill a unique niche in the economy.

One of my roommates from college actually did this. He has three areas of great interest: medicine, sports, and kids. Guess what he became? One of the few doctors in the United States with a specialty in pediatric sports medicine—and he's tremendously successful.

American society has become so specialized that it is common to find subspecialties within specialized fields. Medicine is one example, but it is not the only one. In any area where you know more about a subject than anyone else, you become more valuable than anyone else. The key, of course, is finding a field where your specialty remains relevant to the larger needs of society—and you can keep earning a living from it.

—Richard Thau

CHAPTER 28

How to Get Ahead by Leveraging Everything at Once

If you are successful in your job, your boss may give you a promotion. Or, he or she may not.

One of the strange dynamics of American business is that a company will often go outside the firm to hire a complete stranger and pay that person a salary far in excess of what it would have paid a person promoted from within. Adhering to the "grass is always greener on the other side of the fence" mentality, companies often convince themselves that a magic solution to their needs lurks behind every fresh face that walks in the door.

This may seem unfair, and it is. If you're doing a good job and deserve a promotion, why would your company give the edge to someone from outside? Because that's corporate thinking! But, despite its harshness, you can make this phenomenon work to your advantage. The way to do it is simple: Always be prepared to be mobile—especially while you're in your twenties and unattached. In many cases, you can't get ahead unless you change jobs with some regularity (like once every couple of years).

Let's assume you graduated from college in 1992 and have been holding the same exact job with the same company ever since. What does someone looking at your resume conclude? Not that you've been a dedicated worker who's put in long hours, although that likely is the case. No, what that person sees is an employee who has not been promoted in several years. You want to avoid that judgement at all costs.

You can be promoted from within, but that usually comes by making your superiors know that you want—and can handle—more responsibility. If you're in a company with considerable turnover, it's likely that over the course of four or five years the promotions will come naturally.

But the important question remains: Is this the kind of promotion that you want?

Let's get real. You can't pay your bills with a fancy title alone. If someone tries to promote you by giving you extra responsibilities and a new title, without any increase in pay, that's a big hint that it's time to change jobs because the company is taking advantage of you.

The best situation is one where another company hears about your particular skills and attempts to hire you away. It's not as rare as you think. It even happened to one of us (see sidebar on the next page).

But instead of waiting for the phone to ring, be smart: network.

Follow the instructions in Chapter 8 and get to know as many people as possible in companies where you want to work. Get yourself to trade shows, conferences, and meetings outside your office as often as possible.

Some people say looking for work is a full-time job. It is; it's what you should be doing by networking constantly while you're holding your present job—without actively jeopardizing your present job.

(The names have been changed to protect the guilty and innocent):

On December 12, 1991, I received a call from a person named Jane, who then worked for XYZ, a magazine that competed with my then-employer, PDQ. I knew Jane through industry functions that we both covered as writers, and she told me that a position was opening up at her magazine to do almost exactly what I was doing then. She said that if I was interested, I should call the magazine's editor, Neil, and make plans to meet him.

Later that day, I called his office, and we agreed to meet at 6:45 that evening at a restaurant below Grand Central Station in New York. There we talked over beers for nearly two hours, and he told me that a position was available for a senior reporter to work out of his company's main office in Connecticut.

He asked me whether the fact that the position required a long commute from home would be reason not to consider the job. I told him that I would not look forward to commuting, but I would do it if the financial incentive was sufficient. Since I considered the move a lateral one, there would be no reason to change jobs unless there was more money involved.

In the following days, he contacted me by phone after reading story clips I had sent him, and invited me to meet his editorial director, Anna, on Friday, December 20. This was the first day of my thirteen-day vacation, and I met them at a restaurant on the Upper West Side of Manhattan. We had a cordial meeting during which I suggested to Anna some story ideas, and agreed that I would travel up to Connecticut to see the XYZ offices firsthand on Thursday, December 26.

In the meantime, Neil called me the next day, Saturday, December 21, and surprised me by offering me the job at XYZ for $34,000 per year, $4,000 more than I was going to be making at PDQ starting Jan. 1. (I had, unrelated to this story, just received a tiny raise at PDQ.) I told Neil that I would seriously consider the offer, but could make no announcement that I was leaving PDQ until at least December 30, when my superiors would be returning from vacation.

Well, I was uncertain what to do next. You see, I really did not want to leave PDQ, but wanted to increase my salary closer to its true market value. (Keep in mind that I started there in October 1989 at $28,000 per year, but in neither 1990 nor 1991 did I earn that amount, due to staffwide salary cuts that were needed to keep the magazine going.) Once Neil made his initial overture to me, my goal was for him to follow up with a formal job offer, so that I could get a counteroffer from PDQ. In my heart I was not all that intent on leaving PDQ and taking on some huge commute (one hour and forty-five minutes on four trains—each way), unless the offer was amazingly irresistible. And it wasn't.

My next step was to call my immediate boss, Kevin, and tell him that XYZ had made me an offer. After consulting with my parents, I decided to wait two days, until Monday, December 23, to call Kevin and tell him the news.

Since he was on vacation, I called him at home. He was really surprised to hear the news, but not nearly as surprised as I was when he informed me that the company that owns XYZ, Media Giant, was attempting to lure him away too! And Media Giant was offering him (unlike me) a huge salary increase.

Well, it quickly became apparent to me that Media Giant was trying to put PDQ out of business by luring away its two top writers. Media Giant had tried to buy our magazine, but failed months ago when our owner, Jon, refused to budge. Media Giant, incidentally, owns several media properties and is a huge corporation with very deep pockets. PDQ was not.

Kevin told me that he was leaning toward taking the XYZ offer—and who could blame him, since it represented a huge raise. I said that if he planned to stay, I would be more inclined to leave, knowing that he could replace me. If he planned to leave, then I'd be inclined to stay, since both of us leaving at once would put undue stress on PDQ. Plus, Kevin said, he would recommend that I get his job as editorial director of the magazine.

Kevin called Jon and left a message for him at our main office, but Jon was on vacation and ended up not getting back to Kevin until the following Sunday night, December 29. In the meantime I visited XYZ on Thursday the 26th.

I was supposed to meet Neil at Grand Central Station by the train track, but he wound up not arriving or calling because of an emergency personal matter, and he missed the 8:07 A.M. train. But once I got on the train, I found Anna, and we commuted together, wondering the whole way up what had happened to Neil.

Anyway, XYZ's offices were lovely, despite the fact that they were in a suburban industrial park tucked between a cemetery and a defense contractor. I stayed for a couple of hours, met with the person who would be my immediate boss if I were to join the company, and returned to New York.

The next day I began a five-day trip to Washington, D.C., for New Year's, knowing full well that I would spend part of it talking to Jon from one of my friends' homes down there. And that's what happened.

On Monday morning, I called Kevin in New York, and then Jon in our main office in Massachusetts. Kevin told me that he had spoken to Jon the night before, and informed him that I had been made an offer and that Kevin himself was definitely leaving.

When Jon and I spoke, he told me that Kevin's position was being moved to Massachusetts (PDQ's headquarters), and that he would like me to take it. My response was thanks but no thanks. I had no desire to leave my family and friends and move to suburban Boston, even if it meant a huge raise.

With that matter settled, we moved on to my salary as senior editor. He asked me how much I would have be paid in order to stay. I, being the greedy bastard that I thought I was justified in being after all the pay cuts, said $40,000. He said that was the salary he would pay an executive editor or managing editor, and I was just a senior editor. Then he asked how much XYZ was offering. I said $34,000. He said, "What about $35,000?" I said, "How about $36,000?" He said, "OK, but no more B.S.," meaning no more negotiating with XYZ. I was inclined to agree, but I said to him that if XYZ made a counter-counteroffer that was extremely tempting, I would have to consider it and get back to him.

I then called XYZ and spoke with Anna, and told her the news. She said Neil was away and that I should call him there the next day. On December 31 I did just that, and he said he was disappointed that I opted to stay, and wondered whether I would reconsider the offer if he matched the $36,000 that PDQ was offering. I said no, and explained that there were three main reasons why I declined.

First, I said, I did not want to be responsible for sounding the death knell for PDQ by leaving at the same time as Kevin. Neil had never told me that his company was trying to lure Kevin away simultaneously, and although I didn't say it to Neil, I resented his company's scheming, which seemed like an underhanded way to kill off PDQ. (If Kevin and I both left, it would mean that PDQ would have had no writers who had been there for the previous twelve consecutive months.)

Second, his matching my $36,000 offer was not enticing, since I'd found out that the commute to Connecticut would cost $2,100 per year, meaning that in order to earn that amount in net income, I'd have to earn nearly double that amount in gross salary. In essence, $36,000 at XYZ was considerably less than $36,000 at PDQ, where there was no commutation fee. Moreover, PDQ's New York office was going to be moving to a location within walking distance of my apartment, so I wouldn't have to pay for subways anymore, which would have been another $750 in my pocket every year.

Third, I really did not want to have to commute, no matter what the cost. Neil kept harping on this as my true motivation, though I told him that in and of itself it was not the reason why I turned down his offer. He and Anna despise the commute, they told me, but do it anyway, and talked about either moving the XYZ operation to New York or hiring a car in the meantime to drive the three of us to work. Either way, neither was an immediate remedy, and I could not see spending three and a half hours on eight different trains every day. That became clear when I visited the office on December 26.

(Incidentally, XYZ had a New York bureau, and Kevin was going to be in that office. He knew better than to agree to a commute.)

After speaking to Neil, I called Jon and told him that XYZ had matched his offer, but that I was turning it down. He was relieved and said that now he could enjoy his New Year's Eve.

–Richard Thau

Conclusion

We hope you enjoyed the book. And we hope that we provided some valuable information that will help you get it together by 30.

Remember, when you hit 30, you may not be rich. We're not. You may not be famous. We're not, either. But if you follow our advice seriously, and learn from our personal experiences, we believe that by the time 30 arrives you'll be on your way to being where you want to be over the course of a lifetime.

Remember, you're expected to live a long life. It may seem great to make it early, but there are problems with peaking too early (think of all those child actors who've gone to jail over the past few years, for example). Pace yourself, and you'll find satisfaction on your lifelong journey.

Good luck, and never, ever give up!

Bibliography

Allen, Jeffrey G. *The Resume Makeover: 50 Before-and-After Resumes Teach You How to Create the Most Effective Resume*. New York: Wiley, 1995.

Beatty, Richard H. *The Resume Kit*, 3rd ed. New York: Wiley, 1995.

Bridges, William. *Job Shift: How to Prosper in a Workplace Without Jobs*. New York: Addison-Wesley, 1994.

Burns, Julie Kling. *Opportunities in Computer Systems Careers. Lincolnwood, Ill.:* NTC Publishing Group, 1996.

Dent, Harry S., Jr. *The Great Boom Ahead*. New York: Hyperion, 1993.

———. *The Great Jobs Ahead: Your Comprehensive Guide to Surviving and Prospering in the Coming Work Revolution*. New York: St. Martin's Press, 1995.

Fry, Ron. *Your First Resume: For Students and Anyone Preparing to Enter Today's Tough Job Market*. Franklin Lakes, N.J.: Career Press, 1995.

Gilder, George. *Microcosm*. New York: Simon & Schuster Trade, 1990.

Kleiman, Carol. *The 100 Best Jobs for the 1990s and Beyond*. New York: Berkeley, 1994.

Messmer, Max. *50 Ways to Get Hired*. New York: Morrow, 1995.

Richardson, Bradley. *Jobsmarts for Twentysomethings: A Street-Smart Script for Career Success*. New York: Vintage Books, 1995.

About Third Millennium

Coauthor Richard Thau is the executive director of Third Millennium, a national, nonprofit, nonpartisan organization launched in 1993 by people in their twenties and thirties concerned about the long-term future of the United States.

The group regularly testifies before Congress; gives speeches before college, corporate, and civic organizations; conducts original surveys and studies; sponsors debates; publishes newspaper op-ed articles; and works to raise awareness about economic problems facing our future, such as the national debt and Social Security's pending insolvency.

If you would like to learn more about the organization, please write to: Third Millennium, 817 Broadway, 6th Floor, New York, NY 10003. You can also check out the group's Web site at http://www.thirdmil.org.

Index